FOUNDATION
GCSE Modular Mathematics
for Edexcel

HOMEWORK BOOK

JEAN LINSKY

SERIES EDITOR: ALAN SMITH

Hodder Murray
A MEMBER OF THE HODDER HEADLINE GROUP

Acknowledgements

This high quality material is endorsed by Edexcel and has been through a rigorous quality assurance programme to ensure that it is a suitable companion to the specification for both learners and teachers. This does not mean that its contents will be used verbatim when setting examinations nor is it to be read as being the official specification – a copy of which is available at www.edexcel.org.uk

Hodder Headline's policy is to use papers that are natural, renewable and recyclable products and made from wood grown in sustainable forests. The logging and manufacturing processes are expected to conform to the environmental regulations of the country of origin.

Orders: please contact Bookpoint Ltd, 130 Milton Park, Abingdon, Oxon OX14 4SB. Telephone: (44) 01235 827720. Fax: (44) 01235 400454. Lines are open 9.00 – 5.00, Monday to Saturday, with a 24-hour message answering service. Visit our website at www.hoddereducation.co.uk

© Jean Linsky and Alan Smith 2007
First published in 2007 by
Hodder Murray, an imprint of Hodder Education,
a member of the Hodder Headline Group,
an Hachette Livre UK Company,
338 Euston Road
London NW1 3BH

Personal Tutor CD: © Sophie Goldie, Alan Smith, 2007, with contributions from Andy Sturman; developed by Infuze Limited; cast: Nicolette Landau; recorded at Alchemy Soho.

Impression number   5   4   3   2   1
Year   2012   2011   2010   2009   2008   2007

Cover photo © David Angel @ Début Art
Illustrations © Barking Dog Art
Typeset in 10 point Times Ten Roman by Tech Set Ltd
Printed in Great Britain by Martins of Berwick

A catalogue record for this title is available from the British Library

ISBN: 978 0340 959 152

Contents

Introduction

This Homework Book has been written to support the Hodder Murray Student's Books for the two-tier Edexcel GCSE Modular Mathematics (Foundation Tier) specification and takes into account the withdrawal of coursework from GCSE Mathematics.

The sequence of the material mirrors that of the Student's Books, so that, for example, Exercise 5.2 of the Homework Book provides further practice questions matching the content of Exercise 5.2 in the Student's Book.

Note that the Homework Book includes Chapter 5 and Chapter 6 from the Higher Unit 1, as some centres may wish their Foundation students to take the Higher Handling Data Module as well, in order to boost their overall uniform mark score.

In Unit 2, Stage 1 Exercises are marked with **1** and Stage 2 Exercises are marked with **2**

More practice helps to reinforce the ideas you have learned and makes it easier to remember at a later stage. If, however, you do forget, further help is at hand. As well as the Student's Book, with this book there is also a Personal Tutor CD-ROM. This contains worked examples on key topics to help you recall what you may have forgotten.

Look out for this symbol next to an exercise; it tells you that there is a relevant worked example on the CD-ROM.

All the questions in this book use an icon to show you whether calculators are permitted or not:

 You can use a calculator. Do not use a calculator.

You should follow this advice carefully in order to build up the necessary mixture of calculator and non-calculator skills before the examination.

All of the content of this book has been checked very carefully against the new GCSE specification, to ensure that all examination topics are suitably covered. In addition, practice exam-style papers, with full mark schemes, and the Answers to this homework book, are available in Hodder Murray's accompanying Assessment Pack.

The table below indicates how the Units have been renumbered following the withdrawal of coursework from GCSE Mathematics; the shaded column corresponds to the units in this book.

Specification (Modular) with coursework	Specification (Modular) without coursework
First examination March 2007 and first certification June 2008	First examination March 2008 and first certification June 2009
Unit 1: Internal coursework assessment	No coursework assessment
Unit 2: Handling data	**Unit 1:** Handling data
Unit 3: Number and algebra/Shape, space and measures 1	**Unit 2: Stage 1** (non-calculator multiple choice paper) + **Stage 2** (calculator paper): Number and algebra/Shape, space and measures 1
Unit 4: Number and algebra/Shape, space and measures 2	**Unit 3:** Number and algebra/Shape, space and measures 2

UNIT 1

U1 CHAPTER 1

Collecting data

EXERCISE 1.1

1 Fran carries out a survey.
She wants to see whether the school canteen should be open every day.
She decides to arrive at the canteen at 12 noon and ask the first 50 students who arrive the question:

> 'Don't you agree that our school canteen should stay open every day?'

a) Write down **two** reasons why this is **not** a good way to find out whether students at Fran's school think the school canteen should be open every day.
b) Describe a better method of selecting 50 students that Fran might use.
c) Write down a replacement question that Fran could use.

2 Keith is conducting a survey about restaurants in his town.
Here are three questions in his questionnaire.

   1 How old are you?   _____

   2 What restaurant do you go to?   _____

   3 Do you agree that restaurants are too expensive?
      YES ☐   NO ☐   (Tick one)

a) Explain briefly why each of Keith's questions is unsuitable.
b) Design suitable replacements for each of Keith's questions.

3 Sarah is going to find out about the make-up habits of the female students and teachers at her school.
She has designed three questions:

   1 Are you (Please tick)   Student ☐   Teacher ☐
   2 How old are you?
   3 How much make-up do you use?
      A lot ☐   Not very much ☐

a) Explain briefly why Sarah's questions 2 and 3 are unsuitable.
b) Design suitable replacements for questions 2 and 3 in Sarah's questionnaire.

4 Reeve wants to find out about the amount of pocket money students at her school get.
She has designed three questions.

   1 Who gives you your pocket money?
   2 Who is your favourite sports personality?
   3 How much do you get?   £3–£5   £5–£7   £7 or more

a) Criticise each of Reeve's questions.
b) Design suitable replacements for questions 1 and 3 in Reeve's questionnaire.

5 Fred is carrying out a survey.
He wants to use a questionnaire to find out what pets students at his school like.
He also wants to see if boys like the same pets as girls.
Write down two questions that Fred might use in his questionnaire.

6 Design three suitable questions that Terri might use to test her hypothesis that boys spend more time playing sport than girls.

7 Bella and Victoria are going to interview 52 people at their youth club.
They want to choose the people in as fair a way as possible.

Bella: I'm going to pick the first 52 people that come to the club.

Victoria: Our youth club has 13 groups, so I'm just going to pick four people randomly from each group.

Explain carefully whether one of these methods is better than the other one.

EXERCISE 1.2

State whether the following sets of data would be categorical, discrete or continuous.

1 The number of cars in the school car park.

2 The shoe sizes of the people in your class.

3 The number of hours of television people watch each week.

4 The amount of water people drink in a day.

5 The weight of the contents in customers' shopping trolleys.

6 The heights of the dogs at a dog show.

7 The colours of people's clothes at a concert.

8 The amount waiters earn in tips at a restaurant.

9 The favourite chocolate bar of the students at your school.

10 The number of times a spinner lands on red.

11 The mark that the people in your class scored in a test.

12 The time students take to get to school.

13 The days of the week that people watch television.

14 The volume of water that people use in a bath.

15 The number of days people go abroad in a year.

EXERCISE 1.3

Do not use your calculator for Questions 1–4.

1 Kate carries out a survey about her friends' favourite pets.
She makes a frequency table of her results.

Pet	Tally	Frequency
Cat	|||| |||| ||||	15
Dog	|||| |||	8
Hamster	|||| ||||		
Goldfish	||||	
Birds	||	
Rabbit	|||| |||| |||| |||	

  a) Complete a copy of Kate's frequency table.
  b) How many people liked goldfish best?
  c) Which is the favourite pet of most of Kate's friends?
  d) Which is the least favourite pet of most of Kate's friends?
  e) How many friends did Kate ask altogether?

2 Anna collects data about the flavour of fruit drink people buy in the canteen.
Here are her results.

lemon	mango	apple	lemon	orange	mango
apple	orange	orange	apple	mango	pear
apple	pear	mango	mango	lemon	apple
orange	mango	lemon	lemon	mango	mango
apple	mango	apple	apple	orange	mango

  a) Complete a copy of the frequency table to show Anna's results.

Flavour of drink	Tally	Frequency
apple		
lemon		
mango		
orange		
pear		

  b) Which flavour was the most popular?
  c) How many more people preferred apple to pear?
  d) Which two flavours were equally popular?

3 Lisa has carried out a survey to find out the marks students got in their last test. Here are the marks for the students in her class.

45	55	73	28	87	67	49	52	57	40
20	57	47	92	78	45	61	25	70	42
52	43	41	22	74	74	45	33	62	51

a) Complete the frequency table to show Lisa's results.

Mark	Tally	Frequency
20 and under		
21–30		
31–40		
41–50		
51–60		
61–70		
71–80		
Over 80		

b) How many students got between 41 and 50 marks?
c) How many students scored more than 60 marks?
d) How many students were in Lisa's class?

4 The weights of 36 potatoes were recorded.
The results, in grams, are shown below.

127	163	242	280	339	207	200	97	151	262	190	73
333	310	230	250	222	80	150	328	200	111	102	273
208	212	217	143	349	285	146	174	285	243	291	187

a) Complete the frequency table to show these results.

Weight, w (in g)	Tally	Frequency
$0 < w \leqslant 100$		
$100 < w \leqslant 150$		
$150 < w \leqslant 200$		
$200 < w \leqslant 250$		
$250 < w \leqslant 300$		
$300 < w \leqslant 350$		

b) How many potatoes weighed 200 grams or less?

5 Will collected some data on the number of hours his friends spent on the computer on Sunday.
Here are the times, correct to the nearest hour.

4	2	0	4	4	5	2	3	1	1	5	6
2	1	0	4	4	4	3	1	3	2	1	3

a) Copy and complete the frequency table.

Number of hours	Tally	Frequency
0		
1		
2		
3		
4		
5		
6		

b) How many of Will's friends spent 4 hours, to the nearest hour, on the computer?

c) How many of Will's friends spent more than 4 hours, to the nearest hour, on the computer?

d) How many hours did Will's friends spend on the computer in total?

EXERCISE 1.4

1 Jonathan has been carrying out a survey.
He asked some tea and coffee drinkers whether they drank tea or coffee or both.
Here are some of his results, transferred into a two-way table.

	Tea	Coffee	Both	Total
Male	15			42
Female		12	17	
Total			32	100

  a) Copy and complete the two-way table. **b)** How many females drank only tea?
  c) How many men were in the survey? **d)** How many people drank only coffee?

2 Jess asked 80 people to give their favourite colour from blue, green, red or yellow.
This two-way table shows some of her results.

	Blue	Green	Red	Yellow	Total
Boys			8	6	
Girls	7			2	36
Total	20		31		80

  a) Copy and complete the two-way table.
  b) How many people liked red best?
  c) How many girls liked green best?
  d) How many boys were asked?

3 Jean has collected data on how much weight (w), in kg, people at her slimming club
have lost over the last 6 months.
This two-way table shows some of her results.

		Men	Women	Total
	$0 < w \leqslant 5$	1		10
	$5 < w \leqslant 10$		26	
Weight in kg	**$10 < w \leqslant 15$**		17	27
	over 15	9	11	
	Total	27		

  a) Copy and complete the two-way table.
  b) How many women lost more than 15 kg?
  c) How many men lost more than 10 kg?
  d) How many women lost 10 kg or less?
  e) How many people took part in Jean's survey?

4 The two-way table shows the number of children and the number of pets in some families.

Number of children

		0	1	2	3 or more
Number of pets	**0**	4	4	3	1
	1	3	3	6	5
	2	2	3	4	2
	3 or more	5	1	0	0

a) How many families have 2 children and one pet?
b) How many families have 1 child and two pets?
c) How many families have 3 or more pets?
d) How many families have the same number of children as pets?
e) How many families took part in the survey?

5 The two-way table shows the number of cinemas and the number of large supermarkets in some small towns.

Number of supermarkets

		1	2	3	4
Number of cinemas	**0**	0	7	8	3
	1	2	8	6	4
	2	1	10	15	2
	3	0	6	7	1

a) How many small towns have 4 supermarkets and 2 cinemas?
b) How many small towns have exactly 1 supermarket?
c) How many small towns have the same number of supermarkets as cinemas?
d) How many small towns have fewer supermarkets than cinemas?

6 Mel is carrying out a survey to see whether teachers and students like the same music.
She asks each person in the sample to name their favourite type of music.
Mel records the results on a data collection sheet.
Here are her results after asking the first 14 people.

Pop	Classical	Jazz	Folk	Teachers	Students
JHT II	II	IIII	I	JHT I	JHT III

a) Explain one disadvantage with recording the data in this way.
b) Design an improved data collection sheet that Mel might use.

7 Design a data collection sheet for a survey about how much homework students get.

U1 CHAPTER 2

Working with statistics

EXERCISE 2.1

Do not use your calculator for Questions 1–3.

1 Find: **(i)** the mean, **(ii)** the median and **(iii)** the mode of the following sets of data.

a)	4	4	5	5	8	8	8		
b)	5	7	7	7	11	12	13	14	14
c)	10	10	11	13	16				

2 Pat surveys her friends to find out about their favourite colours.
Here are her results.

red	blue	green	blue	black
green	red	yellow	white	orange
pink	purple	brown	red	black

Which colour is the mode?

3 Mina surveys some students about their favourite subject at school.
Here are her results.

Subject	Frequency
Art	25
Drama	38
English	18
Mathematics	4
Science	2

Which subject is the mode?

You can use a calculator for Questions 4–7.

4 Find: **(i)** the mean, **(ii)** the median and **(iii)** the mode of the following sets of data.

a)	5	2	9	8	0	2	3	7	1		
b)	64	68	75	63	68	74	72	63	78	70	73
c)	125	136	128	130	130	129	120				

5 Find: **(i)** the mean, **(ii)** the median and **(iii)** the mode of the following sets of data.

a)	4	7	9	12	4	2	13	10		
b)	30	38	48	41	25	27	41	38	41	32
c)	43	35	50	31	37	43				

6 Jeremy wants to sell his business.
He puts an advertisement in the local paper.

> **BUSINESS FOR SALE**
> Average annual profit
> £80 000
> Telephone: 8488 5901

Here are his annual profits (to the nearest £10 000) for the past 15 years.

£200 000	£180 000	£150 000	£160 000	£170 000
£140 000	£90 000	£80 000	£60 000	£50 000
£50 000	£40 000	£50 000	£50 000	£30 000

a) Find the mean profit.
b) Find the median profit.
c) Which average has the advertisement used?
Is this a reasonable average to take?
Give a reason for your answer.

7 Joe recorded the temperature at midnight for 12 nights during February.
Here are his results.

2 °C   −5 °C   −4 °C   0 °C   1 °C   −3 °C
−2 °C   1 °C   2 °C   1 °C   −2 °C   −5 °C

Find the:
a) mean temperature   **b)** median temperature   **c)** modal temperature.

EXERCISE 2.2

1. Find: **(i)** the mean, **(ii)** the median, **(iii)** the mode and **(iv)** the range of the following sets of data.

a)	3	7	3	7	7	1	1	7	6	2
b)	13	17	13	17	17	11	11	17	16	12
c)	73	77	73	77	77	71	71	77	76	72
d)	213	217	213	217	217	211	211	217	216	212

e) What do you notice about your answers?

You can use a calculator for Questions 2 and 3.

2 The data set below gives the total number of marks scored by each of 21 students in a test.

67	54	39	63	54	70	43
60	50	64	38	61	87	68
42	55	66	80	33	41	35

a) Work out the range of the data.
b) Write down the mode.
c) Calculate the value of the mean.
d) Find the value of the median.

3 Here are the heights and the weights of 8 students.

Name	Sarah	Rose	Anna	Lisa	Mia	Alison	Jo	Pat
Height	1.5 m	1.27 m	1.42 m	1.67 m	1.27 m	1.4 m	1.61 m	1.56 m
Weight	78.2 kg	95 kg	73.7 kg	85 kg	62.1 kg	80.2 kg	85 kg	62 kg

a) For the heights, work out the:
    (i) mean   **(ii)** median   **(iii)** range.
b) For the weights, work out the:
    (i) mean   **(ii)** median   **(iii)** range.
c) Which person was not very tall but weighed a lot?

EXERCISE 2.3

1 A company sells beds in flat packs for customers to build.
This stem and leaf diagram shows the times, in minutes, it took for each of 14 people to build a bed.

```
2 | 4  5
3 | 3  8  8
4 | 0  1  7  9
5 | 2  5  6
6 | 1  7
```

Key: 2 | 4 = 24

Four more people build a bed from a flat pack.
Their times, in minutes, are 52, 48, 69 and 52
a) Re-draw the stem and leaf diagram and include the four new people.
Using your stem and leaf diagram:
b) Find the mode
c) Find the median
d) Find the range.

2 Patsy has made an unsorted stem and leaf diagram to show the weights, in grams, of 23 loaves of bread in her bakery.

```
70 | 6  4  1
71 | 7  4  0  6  7
72 | 3  9  5  4
73 | 9  8  5  8  3  8
74 | 6  6  4  9  0
```

Key: 70 | 6 = 706

a) Redraw the diagram so that it is fully ordered.
Using your stem and leaf diagram:
b) Find the mode
c) Find the median
d) Find the range.

3 There were 15 pairs of trainers in a sale.
Their prices, in £, are shown below:

23	38	29	53	46	40	23	37
20	34	56	42	33	39	21	

  a) Draw a stem and leaf diagram to show this information.
      Remember to include a key.
  b) Work out the range of the prices.
  c) Find the median price.

4 A cycling group went on a 13-day holiday.
Here are the number of kilometres they planned to cycle each day.

18	32	23	28	19	40	41
25	34	38	19	22	27	

  a) Draw a stem and leaf diagram to show this information.
      (Don't forget the key.)
  b) Work out the range.
  c) Find the median.

5 16 students sat an English examination.
Here are their marks:

72	68	53	60	72	50	83	57
50	75	81	76	65	69	60	71

  a) Draw a stem and leaf diagram to show this information.
  b) Find the median of the marks.

EXERCISE 2.4

1 Alan is an estate agent.
He gathers some data on the number of apartments available in 100 large apartment blocks.

Number of apartments	Frequency
1	28
2	35
3	21
4	9
5	7
Total	100

  a) What is the modal number of apartments available?
  b) Find the median number of apartments available.
  c) Work out the mean number of apartments available.
  d) What is the range of Alan's data?

You can use a calculator for Questions 2 and 3.

2 Lilian conducts a survey.
She finds out how many hours of TV students watched last Monday.
The frequency table shows her results.

a) How many students took
part in Lilian's survey?

The average number of hours of TV watched is 4

Lilian

Number of hours watching TV	Frequency
0	2
1	7
2	9
3	4
4	3
5 or more	0
Total	

b) Explain why Lilian must be wrong.
c) Find the modal number of
hours of TV watched.
d) Find the range of the data.
e) Work out the mean number
of hours of TV watched.
f) Find the median number
of hours of TV watched.

3 Jasmine is surveying the local hockey club.
She records the number of goals scored in
each hockey match in the past three years.

a) How many matches did Jasmine survey?
b) What is the modal number of goals
per match?
c) Find the median number of goals per
match.
d) Work out the mean number of goals
per match.
e) What is the range of Jasmine's data?

Number of goals	Frequency
0	3
1	2
2	5
3	7
4	2
5	3
6	0
7	0
8	1
Total	

EXERCISE 2.5

1 Hajra has measured the weights of some babies and toddlers at a crèche.
The frequency table shows her results.

Weight (w) in kg	Frequency (f)
$0 < w \leqslant 4$	5
$4 < w \leqslant 8$	6
$8 < w \leqslant 12$	7
$12 < w \leqslant 16$	2
$16 < w \leqslant 20$	1
Total	

a) State the modal class.
b) Find the class interval in which the median lies.
c) Estimate the mean weight of these babies and toddlers.
Show all your working clearly.

You can use a calculator for Questions 2–4.

2 Mario records the number of people at the gym each day in April.
The frequency table shows his results.

Number of people at the gym	Frequency	Midpoint
28 to 34	4	
35 to 41	8	
42 to 48	12	
49 to 55	6	
Total		

a) Copy the table, and fill in the midpoint values in the third column.
b) Use the table to help you calculate an estimate of the mean number of people at the gym each day in April.
c) State the modal class.
d) Find the class interval which contains the median.
e) Carlo says, 'The range is 30.'
Explain why Carlo must be wrong.

3 The frequency table shows the ages of the passengers on a cruise liner on the Atlantic.

a) State the modal class.
b) Find the class interval which contains the median.
c) Work out an estimate of the mean age of the passengers on the cruise liner. Give your answer correct to three significant figures.

Age (A) in years	Frequency
$0 < A \leqslant 20$	38
$20 < A \leqslant 40$	70
$40 < A \leqslant 60$	75
$60 < A \leqslant 80$	15
$80 < A \leqslant 100$	2
Total	

4 Seamus solves some Sudoku puzzles.
The frequency table shows the times taken to solve each puzzle.

Time (t) in minutes	Frequency
$5 \leqslant t < 10$	4
$10 \leqslant t < 15$	5
$15 \leqslant t < 20$	7
$20 \leqslant t < 25$	9
$25 \leqslant t < 30$	5
Total	

a) State the modal class.
b) Find the class interval which contains the median.
c) Calculate an estimate of the mean time Seamus took to solve the puzzles.
d) Explain briefly why your answer can only be an estimate.

EXERCISE 2.6

1 Match together these graphs with their descriptions.

P

Q

R

A Length of hair against Height
B Value of car against Age of car
C Height against Weight

2 A park has an outdoor swimming pool.
The scatter graph shows the maximum temperature and the number of people who used the pool on ten Saturdays in summer.

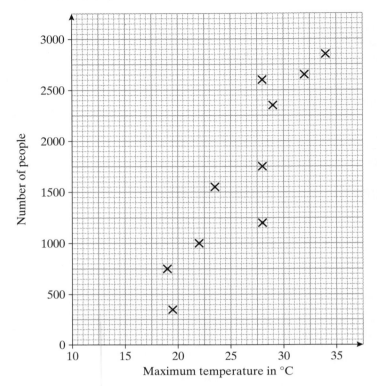

a) Describe the correlation between the maximum temperature and the number of people who used the pool.
b) On a copy of the scatter graph, draw a line of best fit.

The weather forecast for the next Saturday gives a maximum temperature of 27 °C
c) Use your line of best fit to estimate the number of people who will use the pool.

[Edexcel]

3 Some students took a Mathematics test and a Science test.
The scatter graph shows information about the test marks of eight students.

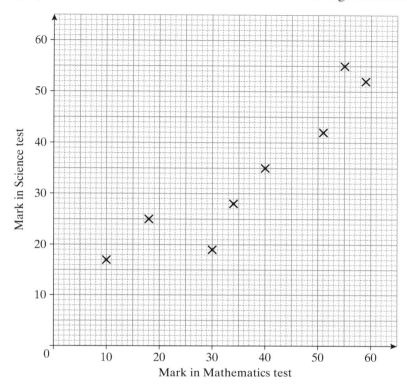

The table shows the test marks of four more students.

Mark in Mathematics test	14	25	50	58
Mark in Science test	21	23	38	51

a) On a copy of the scatter graph, plot the information from the table.
b) Draw a line of best fit on the scatter graph.
c) Describe the **correlation** between the marks in the Mathematics test and the marks in the Science test.

[Edexcel]

4 Ten men took part in a long jump competition.
The table shows the heights of the ten men and the best jumps they made.

Best jump (m)	5.33	6.00	5.00	5.95	4.80	5.72	4.60	5.80	4.40	5.04
Height of men (m)	1.70	1.80	1.65	1.75	1.65	1.74	1.60	1.75	1.60	1.67

a) On a copy of the grid above plot the points as a scatter diagram.
b) Describe the relationship between the height and the maximum difference.
c) Draw in a line of best fit.

[Edexcel]

5 Here is a scatter graph.
One axis is labelled 'Height'.
a) For this graph, state the type
    of correlation.
b) From the list below, choose the most
    appropriate label for the other axis:

   Length of hair
   Number of sisters
   Length of legs
   GCSE French mark

[Edexcel]

6 The scatter graph shows information about twelve athletes.
It shows the time each athlete took to run 100 metres and the length of their best long jump.

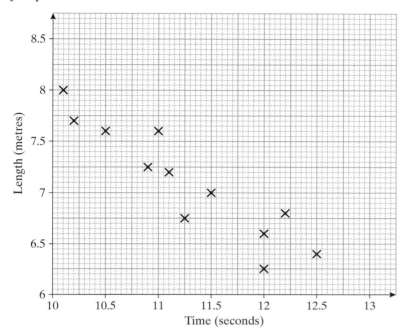

a) Describe the **correlation** between time taken to run 100 metres and length of best long jump.

b) Draw a line of best fit on the scatter graph.

7 a) Here are two scatter graphs, A and B.
For each scatter graph, select the words that best describe the correlation.

	Positive correlation	Negative correlation	No correlation
Scatter graph **A**			
Scatter graph **B**			

U1 CHAPTER 3

Presenting data

EXERCISE 3.1

1 Simone wrote down the favourite colours of all the students in her class.
The bar chart shows her results.

a) Which colour was the favourite for five of the students?

b) Which was the favourite colour?

c) Two colours were equally popular.
Which colours were they?

d) How many students were in Simone's class?

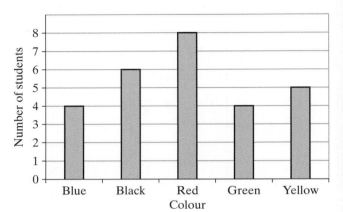

2 A superstore uses a pictogram to show the number of DVD players they sold over a 4-week period.

a) How many DVD players were sold in week 1?

b) In which week were the least number of DVD players sold?

c) How many DVD players were sold in week 3?

d) How many DVD players were sold in week 4?

Key: ⊞ = 4 DVD players

Week 1	⊞ ⊞ ⊞
Week 2	⊞ ⊞
Week 3	⊞ ⊟
Week 4	⊞ ⊞ ⊞ ⊞
Week 5	
Week 6	

The superstore has data for two more weeks.

Week number	Number of DVD players sold
Week 5	16
Week 6	9

e) Add the data to a copy of the pictogram.

3 Fatima recorded the maximum temperatures in London and in Cape Town for the first six months of last year.
She produced a bar chart to compare the temperatures in the two cities.

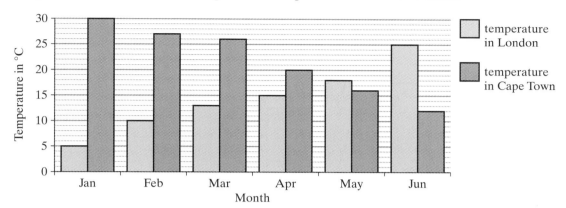

Use the dual bar chart to write down the following.
a) the maximum temperature in February in:
   (i) London   **(ii)** Cape Town
b) the month which had the highest maximum temperature in:
   (i) London   **(ii)** Cape Town
c) the month where the difference in maximum temperature between the two cities was:
   (i) the highest   **(ii)** the lowest
   and write down what this difference was.
d) the month where the highest maximum temperature in London became greater than the highest maximum temperature in Cape Town.

4 An art gallery had a sale of paintings.
The owner wrote down her total sales on each of the first five days of the sale.
The information is in the table below.

Day of the sale	Total sales
Monday	£4000
Tuesday	£3000
Wednesday	£1500
Thursday	£2250
Friday	£3750

Draw a pictogram to show this information.

Use ⊕ to represent £1000

5 Six students, Ann, Ben, Con, Dani, Ed and Flo, each sat an examination in English, Mathematics and Science.
Each examination was marked out of 100
Their teacher made a bar chart of their results.

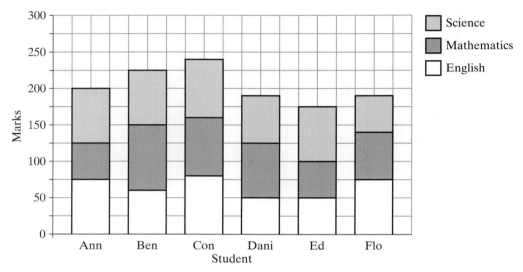

a) Which student got the highest total mark?
b) Which student got the highest Mathematics mark?
c) Two students got the same overall total.
   Write down the names of these two students.
d) One student got the same mark for all three subjects.
   Write down the name of this student.
e) What did Ann score for Science?
f) One student's best mark was for English.
   Write down the name of this student.

6 May counts the number of each of her favourite animals at the zoo.
Here are her results.

Type of animal	Number of animals
Giraffes	3
Lions	6
Monkeys	10
Polar Bears	3
Zebras	8

Draw a bar chart to show this information.

EXERCISE 3.2

1 Des asked 40 of his friends which was their favourite holiday destination in the UK. The table shows the results.

Draw a pie chart to illustrate this information.

City	Frequency
Blackpool	5
Bournemouth	7
Brighton	10
Falmouth	2
London	16

2 An optometrist wrote down what he sold to the 18 patients he saw on Saturday.

Draw a pie chart to illustrate this information.

Sales	Number
Spectacles	12
Contact lenses	4
Nothing	2

3 Patsy earns £30 a week doing various jobs. The table shows how she spent this money last week.

Draw a pie chart to illustrate this information.

Cinema	£7
Clothes	£12
Eating out	£8
Magazines	£3

4 Richard has 60 books on the bookshelves in his room.

Draw a pie chart to illustrate this data.

Type of book	Number of books
Science Fiction	17
Adventure	7
Reference	15
Novel	21

5 The table shows the spread of the ages of the members of a sports club.

Draw a pie chart to illustrate this data.

Age of members	Percentage
under 18	10
$18 \leqslant age < 25$	18
$25 \leqslant age < 40$	42
$40 \leqslant age < 60$	22
60 or over	8

6 Craig draws a pie chart to show how he uses his earnings in a typical month.

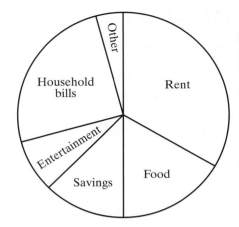

  a) On what does he spend the most money?

  Craig earns £720 per month after tax.

  b) Work out how much Craig spends on:
     (i) household bills
     (ii) entertainment
     (iii) rent
     (iv) food

  c) How much does Craig save each month?

7 Janet and John each draw a pie chart to show how long they spent on their homework last weekend.

Janet spends 6 hours on her homework.
John spends 8 hours on his homework.

  a) Write down the subject which is the mode for:
     (i) Janet   **(ii)** John

  b) Work out how much time Janet spends on:
     (i) Maths   **(ii)** Art

  c) Work out how much time John spends on Science.

  d) Max says that Janet spends longer on her History homework than John because the angle for History on her pie chart is larger than the angle for History on John's pie chart.
  Explain why Max is wrong.

EXERCISE 3.3

Do not use your calculator for Questions 1 and 2.

1 Here are the ages of the people staying in a hotel.
   a) Draw a frequency diagram to show this data.
   b) How many people were staying in the hotel?
   c) Write down the modal class interval.

Age	Frequency
$0 \leqslant$ age < 15	15
$15 \leqslant$ age < 30	11
$30 \leqslant$ age < 45	47
$45 \leqslant$ age < 60	32
$60 \leqslant$ age < 75	10
$75 \leqslant$ age < 90	4

2 Lara carries out a survey to find out the average amount of time students spend watching TV at the weekend.
Here are her results.
Draw a histogram of Lara's results.

Time in hours (h)	Frequency
$0 \leqslant h < 3$	5
$3 \leqslant h < 6$	14
$6 \leqslant h < 9$	22
$9 \leqslant h < 12$	8

You can use your calculator for Questions 3 and 4.

3 Maddy carried out a survey of the time, in minutes, it took students to get to school. The table shows the results of her survey.
   a) Draw a histogram to show this data.
   b) Write down the modal class interval.
   c) How many students were in Maddy's survey?
   d) How many students took less than half an hour to get to school?

Time, t, in minutes	Frequency
$0 \leqslant t < 10$	11
$10 \leqslant t < 20$	34
$20 \leqslant t < 30$	26
$30 \leqslant t < 40$	15
$40 \leqslant t < 50$	4

   e) Find an estimate for the mean time, in minutes, it took students to get to school.

4 A vet recorded the weight of 60 animals he saw over the weekend.
   a) Draw a histogram to show this data.
   b) Write down the modal class interval.
   c) Estimate the mean weight of the animals.
   d) Write down the class interval which contains the median.

Weight, w, in kg	Frequency
$0 \leqslant w < 3$	14
$3 \leqslant w < 6$	8
$6 \leqslant w < 9$	10
$9 \leqslant w < 12$	12
$12 \leqslant w < 15$	16

EXERCISE 3.4

1 Draw a frequency polygon for each of the sets of data given in Exercise 3.3

You can use your calculator for Questions 2 and 3.

2 A football club carried out a survey of the ages of its 274 supporters at a football match. The results of the survey are shown in the table.

Age group, x years	Frequency
$0 \leqslant x < 10$	24
$10 \leqslant x < 20$	36
$20 \leqslant x < 30$	60
$30 \leqslant x < 40$	52
$40 \leqslant x < 50$	30
$50 \leqslant x < 60$	44
$60 \leqslant x < 70$	28

a) Draw a frequency polygon to show this information.
b) Which is the modal class?
c) Find the class interval which contains the median.
d) Find an estimate for the mean age.

3 Stan measured the heights of 60 boxes.
Each height was recorded.
The table shows information about these height.

Height (h cm)	Frequency
$0 < h \leqslant 20$	11
$20 < h \leqslant 40$	20
$40 < h \leqslant 60$	7
$60 < h \leqslant 80$	22

a) Draw a frequency polygon to show this information.
b) Work out an estimate for the mean height of these boxes.
c) Write down the modal class interval.
d) Find the class interval that contains the median.

EXERCISE 3.5

1 Lauren spent a year travelling.
She had a plane ticket to fly to
12 different countries in any order.
Each month she went to a different
country and recorded the
temperature there, in °C, on the
10th day of each month.
The graph shows this information.

a) What is the range of the
temperatures?
b) Write down the temperature in:
   (i) July   **(ii)** September.
c) Lauren takes two more readings:

Month	Nov	Dec
Temp	−5 °C	27 °C

Add these measurements to a copy of Lauren's graph.

2 The time-series graph shows the
takings of a small company
one year.

a) What is the range of the
takings?
b) Which two months have the
same takings?
c) Here is the data for November
and December.

Month	Nov	Dec
Takings	£4500	£5700

Add the data to a copy of the time-series graph.

3 Mr Smith recorded the number of customers in his shop at particular times one Friday.
Here are his results.

Time	9 am	10 am	11 am	12 noon	1 pm	2 pm	3 pm	4 pm	5 pm
No. customers	3	5	6	5	8	9	6	4	2

Draw a time-series graph for this data.

U1 CHAPTER 4

Probability

EXERCISE 4.1

1 The colours on a regular 5-sided spinner
are red, blue, yellow, green and purple.
Dean spins the spinner once.
Find the probability that it
   a) lands on red
   b) does **not** land on green
   c) lands on black.

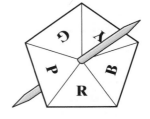

2 A football team is equally likely to win, lose or draw a match.
On a copy of the probability line below mark with a letter **W** the probability that the
football team will win a match.

3 A fair dice has sides numbered 1, 2, 3, 4, 5 and 6
The dice is thrown once.
On a copy of the probability line below:

   a) mark with a letter **A** the probability that the dice will land on an **even** number
   b) mark with a letter **B** the probability that the dice will land on a number **bigger** than 4
   c) mark with a letter **C** the probability that the dice will **not** land on a number bigger
   than 4
   d) mark with a letter **D** the probability that the dice will land on a number **bigger** than 0
   e) mark with a letter **E** the probability that the dice will land on a number **smaller** than 1

4 A regular eight-sided spinner has sides 1, 2, 3, 4, 5, 6, 7 and 8
The spinner is spun once.
On a copy of the probability line below:

   a) mark with a letter **A** the probability that the spinner will
   land on an odd number
   b) mark with a letter **B** the probability that the spinner will land on a 5
   c) mark with a letter **C** the probability that the spinner will land on a number less than 10
   d) mark with a letter **D** the probability that the spinner will land on a factor of 15
   e) mark with a letter **E** the probability that the spinner will **not** land on a number less
   than 4
   f) mark with a letter **F** the probability that the spinner will land on a number bigger
   than 2

5 The probability that Deborah wins a competition is 0.27
What is the probability that Deborah does not win the competition?

6 A bag contains 27 balls.
There are 10 blue balls and 13 red balls.
The rest of the balls are black.
A ball is chosen at random.
Find the probability that this ball is
   a) red   **b)** **not** blue   **c)** black.

7 The probability that I will be at school tomorrow is 0.93
Work out the probability that I will **not** be at school tomorrow.

8 A drawer contains 40 socks.
10 of them are black, the rest are white or grey.
There are four times as many white socks as grey socks.
A sock is chosen at random.
   a) Work out the probability that it is black.
   b) Work out the probability that it is **not** black.
   c) Work out the probability that it is white.

EXERCISE 4.2

Do not use your calculator for Questions 1 and 2.

1 The diagram on the right shows some shapes.

   a) Copy and complete the table to show the number of shapes in each category.

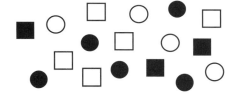

	Black	White	Total
Square			
Circle			
Total			

One of the shapes is chosen at random.
   b) Write down the probability that the shape is a circle.
   c) Write down the probability that the shape is **not** black.
   d) Write down the probability that the shape is a black square.

2 The two-way table shows some information about the numbers of people in a library.
   a) Copy and complete the two-way table.
A person in the library chooses a book.
   b) Work out the probability that the person is a child.
One of the people in the library uses the computer.
   c) Work out the probability that the person is male.

	Adults	Children	Total
Male		7	18
Female	20		
Total			50

You can use your calculator for Questions 3 and 4.

3 A small play group has children aged 2 years, 3 years and 4 years. Darren wrote down the ages of the children that attended on Tuesday. The two-way table shows the results.

	2 years	3 years	4 years	Total
Boys	5	9	5	19
Girls	6	5	7	18
Total	11	14	12	37

a) Find the probability that a child is a 2-year-old girl.
b) Find the probability that a 4-year-old is a boy.
c) Find the probability that a child is a 3-year-old.

4 A restaurant serves fruit salad, cheesecake or mousse for dessert.
Mr Chen keeps a record of what he serves on Sunday.
Every customer had one dessert.
The table shows some of this information.

	Fruit Salad	Cheesecake	Mousse	Total
Midday	10			
Evening		8		46
Total	28		25	70

a) Copy and complete the two-way table.
b) Find the probability that a customer had cheesecake for dessert.
c) Find the probability that a customer had mousse for dessert in the evening.

EXERCISE 4.3

1 Two fair spinners are spun together. One spinner has five sides and the other has seven sides. The scores are **added** together.

a) Copy and complete the table to show all the possible outcomes.
b) What is the total number of possible outcomes?
c) Write down the probability of getting a total of:
  (i) 9 (ii) 6
  (iii) 11 (iv) **not** 7
  (v) an even number (vi) 10 or more

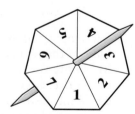

+	1	2	3	4	5	6	7
1	2						
2				6			
3		5					10
4							
5				9			12

2 A fair coin and a fair five-sided spinner
are thrown together.

   a) Write down all the possible outcomes of throwing
the fair coin and the fair spinner.

   b) Write down the probability of getting:

     (i) a 'head' and a 'D'   **(ii)** a 'tail' and **not** a C.

3 Two fair spinners are spun together.
One spinner has five sides and the
other has eight sides.

The scores are **multiplied** together.

   a) Copy and complete the table to
show all the possible outcomes.

   b) What is the total number of possible
outcomes?

   c) Write down the probability of
getting a total of:

     (i) 12

     (ii) 130

     (iii) 24

     (iv) **not** 18

     (v) an odd number

     (vi) 25 or more.

×	1	2	3	4	5	6	7	8
1	1							
2						12		
3		6					21	
4					20			
5								40

4 Gloria eats dinner in a restaurant.
She randomly selects a starter, a main
course and a dessert from this list.

   a) List all the possible outcomes of
randomly selecting a starter, a
main course and a dessert.

   b) Write down the probability that Gloria will eat:

     i) pâté   **(ii)** soup and chicken   **(iii)** pâté, lamb and cherry pie.

Starter	Main course	Dessert
Soup	Chicken	Cherry pie
Pâté	Lamb	Fruit salad

5 Two fair spinners are spun together.
One spinner has four sides and the other has
six sides.

The **difference** between the two scores is found.

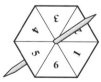

   a) Complete the table to show all the
possible outcomes.

   b) What is the total number of
possible outcomes?

   c) Write down the probability of
getting a total of:

     (i) 1

     (ii) 5

     (iii) 2

     (iv) **not** 0

     (v) an even number

     (vi) 4 or less

Difference	1	2	3	4	5	6
1	0					
2			1			
3				2		
4	3					

6 Liz picks one shape from Box P.
She then picks one shape from Box Q.

One pair she could pick is (white rectangle, white circle).

a) List all the pairs Liz could pick.
b) What is the probability that Liz picks (white rectangle, black circle)?
c) What is the probability that Liz picks a white circle?
d) What is the probability that Liz picks two circles?

7 Geoff picks one number from each of Boxes A, B and C.
One trio he could pick is (2, 4, 1)

A	B	C
9	4	5 7
2	8	1

a) List all the trios Geoff could pick.
b) Write down the probability that:
   (i) Geoff picks (2, 4, 1)   **(ii)** Geoff picks a '7'   **(iii)** Geoff picks an '8'
   (iv) Geoff picks a '9' and a '5'   **(v)** Geoff picks three numbers that total 24

EXERCISE 4.4

Do not use your calculator for Questions 1–4.

1 The probability that Jean is late for work is 0.1
How many times would you expect Jean to be late for work in 30 working days?

2 A fair coin is thrown 300 times.
How many times would you expect it to show 'heads'?

3 Simon has a biased dice.
Simon tosses the dice 100 times.
Here are his results.

Result	1	2	3	4	5	6
Frequency	42	27	2	3	21	5

Write down the experimental probability of the dice landing on:
a) 5   **b)** 1   **c)** an odd number

4 The probability of a biased coin showing 'heads' is 0.25
a) What is the probability of the coin showing 'tails'?

The coin is thrown 40 times.
b) Work out an estimate for the number of times it will show 'tails'.

You can use your calculator for Questions 5–8.

5 The probability that Colin will put up his hand in a lesson is $\frac{4}{5}$
   a) What is the probability that Colin will not put up his hand in a lesson?
   Colin goes to 40 lessons each week.
   b) Work out an estimate for the number of times Colin will put up his hand in a week.

6 There are 500 sweets in a jar. 100 of the sweets are red.
   The rest are orange, yellow or green.
   Ted takes a sweet at random from the jar and puts it back.
   a) Calculate the probability that Ted takes a red sweet.
   Tessa takes 50 sweets at random from the jar.
   20 of these sweets are orange.
   b) Estimate how many orange sweets are in the jar.

7 A box contains just 1p coins, 2p coins and 5p coins.
   There are 200 coins in the box and 50 of these are 2p coins.
   Miriam randomly takes a coin from the box and then puts it back.
   a) Work out the probability that the coin Miriam takes is a 2p coin.
   Miriam then randomly takes 40 coins from the box. 10 of these were 5p coins.
   b) Estimate the total number of 5p coins in the box.

8 In the sixth form at Gravitas School there are 63 boys and 78 girls.
   a) A student is chosen at random from the sixth form.
      Work out the probability that the student is a girl.
   b) There are 1200 students altogether at Gravitas School.
      Estimate the total number of girls at the school.
   c) Explain why your estimate might not be very reliable.

EXERCISE 4.5

1 When Lara returns from school she either does her homework or watches TV or tidies her room or has a snack.
   The probability that Lara does her homework is 0.2
   The probability that Lara watches TV is 0.4
   The probability that Lara has a snack is 0.3
   What is the probability that Lara tidies her room?

2 Joan either has coffee or tea or hot chocolate in the morning.
   The probability that Joan has coffee is 0.4
   The probability that Joan has tea is 0.25
   What is the probability that Joan has hot chocolate in the morning?

3 Traffic lights show either red or amber or green.
   The probability that the traffic lights show red is 0.43
   The probability that the traffic lights show green is 0.46
   a) What is the probability that the traffic lights show amber?
   There are 20 traffic lights on Janet's way to work.
   b) Work out an estimate for the number of times the traffic lights will show green.

4 A bag contains black, white, pink and orange counters.
A counter is drawn at random.
The table shows the probabilities of the counter being each of the four colours.

Colour	Black	White	Pink	Orange
Probability	$\frac{8}{23}$		$\frac{3}{23}$	$\frac{2}{23}$

   a) What is the probability of the counter being white?
   b) What is the probability of the counter being black or pink?
   c) What is the probability of the counter **not** being orange?

5 A biased dice shows scores of 1, 2, 3, 4, 5, 6 with these probabilities.

Score	1	2	3	4	5	6
Probability	0.23		0.3	0.18	0.1	0.05

The dice is rolled once. Find the probability that the score obtained is:
   a) 2   **b)** not 4   **c)** 5 or 6   **d)** an odd number.

6 When Andrew goes to work he is either early, on time or late.
The incomplete table shows some probabilities.

	Early	On time	Late
Probability	$\frac{27}{100}$		$\frac{6}{100}$

   a) What is the probability that Andrew arrives on time?
   b) Which of the three outcomes is most likely?
   c) Find the probability that Andrew is **not** late for work.

7 There are four types of animals I might see in my garden.
The table shows the probability that a fox or a hedgehog or a squirrel or a
cat will be seen in my garden. No two animals are ever in the garden at the same time.

Type of creature	Fox	Hedgehog	Squirrel	Cat
Probability	0.15		0.4	0.28

   a) Copy and complete the probability table.
   b) Which type of animal do I see most often in my garden?

An animal is observed at random.
Find the probability that:
   c) it is **not** a cat,
   d) it is a fox or a squirrel.

8 Bertha has three children, Robert, Johnny and Stephen.
Every Friday night Bertha has dinner with one of her children.
The probability that she has dinner with Robert is 0.28 and the probability
that she has dinner with Johnny is 0.3
   a) Work out the probability that she has dinner with Stephen.
   b) Work out the probability that she does **not** have dinner with Stephen.

9 A biased spinner gives scores of 1, 2, 3 or 4
The probability of getting 1 is 0.37
The probability of getting 2 is 0.18
The probability of getting 4 is 0.2
a) Calculate the probability of getting an even score.
b) Work out the probability of getting a score of 3

10 Sue often partners Janet or Don at tennis.
The probability that she will partner Janet is 0.38
The probability that she will partner Don is 0.17
a) Work out the probability that she will partner Janet or Don at tennis.
b) Work out the probability that she will **not** partner either of these two at tennis.

11 Alex goes to the cinema.
He can choose from a comedy, a drama, a science fiction movie or a horror movie.
The table shows the probability that Alex will choose a particular type of movie.

Type of movie	Comedy	Drama	Science fiction	Horror
Probability	0.17	0.23	x	x

a) Find the probability that he chooses a comedy or a drama.
b) Find the probability that he chooses a science fiction movie or a horror movie.

The probability he will choose to see a science fiction movie is the same as the probability he will choose to see a horror movie.
c) Find the probability he will choose to see a horror movie.

12 The junior football team at Roddington School is picked from students in Years 7 or 8 or 9
Mr Right selects the junior football teams. The probability that he might select a student from Years 7 or 8 is shown in the table below.

Year group	Year 7	Year 8	Year 9
Probability	24%	32%	

a) Copy and complete the probability table.
Mr Right needs to pick 50 students for some junior football teams.
b) Estimate the number of Year 8 students he is likely to pick.

13 A drawer contains black, white, blue and brown socks.
In a probability experiment, one sock is chosen at random, and removed from the drawer.
Its colour is noted, and it is returned to the drawer.
The table shows some probabilities for this experiment.

Colour	Black	White	Blue	Brown
Probability	0.36	0.31	0.1	

a) Find the probability of choosing a brown sock.
The experiment is carried out 300 times.
b) Estimate the number of times a white sock is chosen.

U1 CHAPTER 5

Further statistics (Higher Tier only)

EXERCISE 5.1

1 The table shows the number of children in each of 4 groups at a club.

A stratified sample of size 40 is to be taken from the club.

Alix says that this means you take 10 from each group.

(i) Explain why Alix is wrong.
(ii) Work out how many students from each group should be in the sample.

Group	Number of children
A	27
B	38
C	13
D	25

2 A newspaper editor wants to find out people's opinions about a law that has just been passed in Parliament.

Reporter A — I'm going to write an article about the law and invite readers of the paper to write in and express their views about the new law.

Reporter B — I'm going to stand in the street and ask every tenth person what they think of the new law.

Explain which of these methods is the better one.

3 Davin is studying the number of matches in boxes of Rover matches.
He wants to see if the number of matches in each box is the same.
He goes to his local newsagent and buys 50 boxes of Rover matches.
He then takes them home and counts the numbers in each box.
Explain briefly whether you think this is a good sampling method.

4 The table shows the number of students in each year group at Wendower School.
There are 800 students at the school altogether.

Age group	Year 7	Year 8	Year 9	Year 10	Year 11
Number of students	185	199	226	82	108

Mavis wants to take a stratified sample of 60 students from the school.
Draw up a table to show how many students she should select from each year group.

5 David and Graham are planning a coursework exercise.
They want to find out about the student absences at different schools in London.

I'm going to sample four schools in each borough.

David

I'm going to sample 30% of the schools in London.

Graham

Explain why one of these methods is much better than the other.

 EXERCISE 5.2

1 320 students took a test.
The cumulative frequency graph gives information about their marks.

Work out an estimate for the interquartile range of their marks.

[Edexcel]

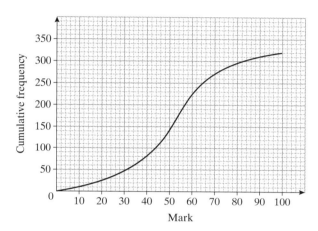

2 Bill asked 80 students how many hours each of them spent doing homework last week.
He used the information to draw this cumulative frequency graph.

Use the cumulative frequency graph to find an estimate for:
a) the median number of hours
b) the number of students who spent more than 7 hours on their homework. [Edexcel]

3 The cumulative frequency diagram below gives information about the prices of 120 houses.
a) Find an estimate for the number of houses with prices less than £130 000
b) Work out an estimate for the interquartile range of the prices of the 120 houses.

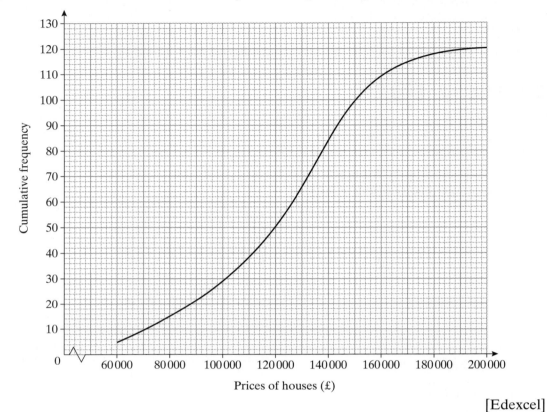

Prices of houses (£)

[Edexcel]

4 The table shows information about the number of hours that 120 children used a computer last week.

Number of hours (h)	Frequency
$0 < h \leqslant 2$	10
$2 < h \leqslant 4$	15
$4 < h \leqslant 6$	30
$6 < h \leqslant 8$	35
$8 < h \leqslant 10$	25
$10 < h \leqslant 12$	5

a) Complete a copy of the cumulative frequency table.

Number of hours (h)	Cumulative frequency
$0 < h \leqslant 2$	10
$2 < h \leqslant 4$	
$4 < h \leqslant 6$	
$6 < h \leqslant 8$	
$8 < h \leqslant 10$	
$10 < h \leqslant 12$	

b) On a copy of the grid, draw a cumulative frequency graph for your table.

c) Use your graph to find an estimate for the number of children who used a computer for **less** than 7 hours last week.   [Edexcel]

5 The cumulative frequency table gives information about the heights, in centimetres, of some students at Bax School.

a) On a grid, with the horizontal axis having heights from 135 cm to 175 cm and the vertical axis having a cumulative frequency of 0 to 180, draw a cumulative frequency graph for the data in the table.

b) Use your cumulative frequency graph to estimate:
  (i) the median height
  (ii) the number of students with height less than 151 cm

Heights (h) of students in cm	Cumulative frequency
$h < 135$	0
$135 \leqslant h < 140$	2
$135 \leqslant h < 145$	10
$135 \leqslant h < 150$	29
$135 \leqslant h < 155$	70
$135 \leqslant h < 160$	115
$135 \leqslant h < 165$	143
$135 \leqslant h < 170$	156
$135 < h \leqslant 175$	163

6 Here are four cumulative frequency diagrams.

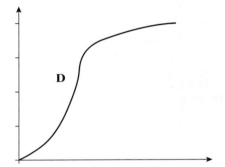

Here are four box plots.

For each box plot, write down the letter of the appropriate cumulative frequency diagram.

P and ....

Q and ....

R and ....

S and ....

EXERCISE 5.3

1. 7 cats have a mean weight of 3.4 kg. Another cat weighs 4.2 kg
   Work out the mean weight of all 8 cats.

2. 10 pieces of cheese have a mean weight of 320 g
   Another 8 pieces of cheese have a mean weight of 545 g
   Work out the mean weight of all 18 pieces of cheese.

3. There are 15 players in a football team.
   6 of the players have a mean height of 1.7 m
   The other 9 players have a mean height of 1.62 m
   Find the mean height for all 15 players.

4. There are 400 students at a school. The students take a Mathematics exam.
   The table below shows the results.

	Number of students	Mean mark
Girls	230	63%
Boys	170	67%

   Calculate the mean mark for all 400 students.

5. The mean number of children in 7 families in a street is 2.8 children.
   The mean number of children in the 7 families in the next street is 1.75 children.

   Leo says, 'The mean number of children in all 14 families is $\dfrac{2.8 + 1.75}{2} = 2.275$ children.'

   Explain carefully whether Leo is right or wrong.

6. The mean weight loss of the 25 adults at a slimming class on Monday was 1.72 kg
   Another adult arrived late and after he was weighed the mean increased to 1.74 kg
   Work out the weight loss of the adult who arrived late.

7. To get a distinction, Katrina has to get an average of 80 marks over 10 examinations.
   In the first 9 examinations Katrina obtained a mean score of 81 marks.
   Work out the least number of marks she needs to score in the tenth examination in order to obtain a distinction.

8. One year the mean monthly rainfall in a city in India was 10 cm
   The mean monthly rainfall for the first 7 months was only 5 cm
   Work out the mean monthly rainfall for the next 5 months.

EXERCISE 5.4 pt

1 The table shows the number of umbrellas sold each quarter by a small shop.
The data was collected from January 1997 to December 1999

1997				1998				1999			
Jan to Mar	Apr to Jun	Jul to Sep	Oct to Dec	Jan to Mar	Apr to Jun	Jul to Sep	Oct to Dec	Jan to Mar	Apr to Jun	Jul to Sep	Oct to Dec
27	15	10	20	28	14	11	21	30	16	13	22
	18	18.25	18								

a) Work out the four-quarter moving averages for the data.
The first three have been done for you.
b) Plot a time series graph of the original data.
c) On the same axes, plot a time series graph of the moving averages.
What do the graphs show you about the seasonal variation in the number of umbrellas sold?

2 The table shows the number of absences at a school over a period of three weeks.

Week 1					Week 2					Week 3				
Mon	Tue	Wed	Thu	Fri	Mon	Tue	Wed	Thu	Fri	Mon	Tue	Wed	Thu	Fri
18	10	7	6	16	20	13	8	8	18	21	14	8	10	20
		11.4	11.8	12.4										

a) Work out the five-day moving averages for the data.
Explain why there are only 11 of these values, not 15
The first three have been done for you.
b) Plot a time series graph of the original data.
What can you say about the absences on different days of the week?
c) Plot a time series graph of the moving averages.
What can you say about the weekly average absences?

3 The table shows the average number of school dinners sold each day by the school canteen over a period of four years.

Year	2001			2002			2003			2004		
Term	1st	2nd	3rd	1st	2nd	3rd	1st	2nd	3rd	1st	2nd	3rd
	150	127	101	138	121	89	135	118	86	132	109	77
		126	122	120								

a) Plot a time series graph of the data.
Describe whether you can see any seasonal variation in the number of school dinners sold.
b) Calculate a set of three-value moving averages from the data.
Three of the ten values have been done for you.
c) Plot a time series graph of the moving averages.
d) Add a straight line to your graph to indicate the underlying trend.

EXERCISE 5.5

1 Justin is a florist.

He measured 100 flowers and recorded the heights to the nearest centimetre.
The table shows information about the heights, h, of the 100 flowers.

Height, h	Frequency, f
$0 \leqslant h < 20$	24
$20 \leqslant h < 40$	38
$40 \leqslant h < 60$	16
$60 \leqslant h < 80$	12
$80 \leqslant h < 100$	10

a) Draw a frequency polygon to show this information.
Use graph paper with the *frequency* axis 8 cm high, numbered from 0 to 40, and the *height* axis 10 cm wide, numbered from 0 to 100

b) Work out an estimate for the mean height of these flowers.

c) Find the class interval that contains the median.

2 The table gives information about how long, in minutes, some people took to read a magazine.

Time (t) in minutes	Frequency
$0 < t \leqslant 10$	20
$10 < t \leqslant 15$	30
$15 < t \leqslant 30$	60
$30 < t \leqslant 60$	90

Use the table to draw a histogram that shows this information.

3 A teacher asked some Year 10 students how long they spent doing homework each night. The histogram was drawn from this information.

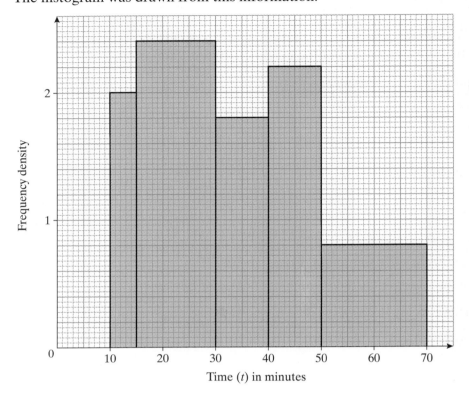

Time (t) in minutes

Use the histogram to complete the table.

Time (t) in minutes	Frequency
$10 \leqslant t < 15$	10
$15 \leqslant t < 30$	
$30 \leqslant t < 40$	
$40 \leqslant t < 50$	
$50 \leqslant t < 70$	

4 A teacher asked some students how much time they spent using a mobile phone one week. The histogram was drawn from this information.

Use the histogram to complete a copy of the table.

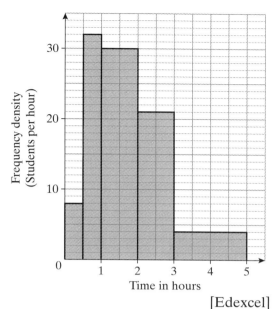

Time (t) in hours	Frequency
$0 \leqslant t < \frac{1}{2}$	
$\frac{1}{2} \leqslant t < 1$	
$1 \leqslant t < 2$	30
$2 \leqslant t < 3$	
$3 \leqslant t < 5$	

[Edexcel]

5 Some students at Highfliers School took a Mathematics examination. The unfinished table and histogram show some information about their marks.

Mark ($x\%$)	Frequency
$0 < x \leqslant 40$	10
$40 < x \leqslant 60$	40
$60 < x \leqslant 75$	45
$75 < x \leqslant 85$	60
$85 < x \leqslant 95$	
$95 < x \leqslant 100$	25

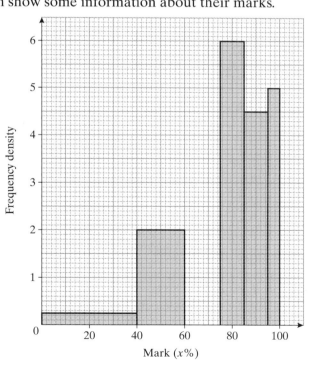

a) Use the information in the table to complete a copy of the histogram.
b) Use the information in the histogram to complete the table. [Edexcel]

U1 CHAPTER 6

Further probability (Higher Tier only)

EXERCISE 6.1

1 A box contains coins. A coin is chosen at random.
   The table shows the probabilities of the coin being of a certain value.

Value	1p	5p	10p	20p	50p
Probability	0.1	0.35	0.2	0.05	0.3

   Find the probability that the chosen coin is:
   a) a 10p coin
   b) a 20p or 50p coin
   c) not a 5p coin.

2 A spinner can land on Red, Blue, Pink, Green or Black.
   The table shows the probabilities that the spinner will land on Red, Blue, Pink or Green.

Colour	Red	Blue	Pink	Green	Black
Probability	0.25	0.1	0.3	0.14	

   Find the probability that the spinner lands on:
   a) Pink
   b) Blue or Green
   c) Black

3 Debbie partners either Ivan, Joshua or Leo in a game.
   The probability that she will partner Ivan is 0.4
   The probability that she will partner Leo is 0.5
   Work out the probability that in a game Debbie will partner:
   a) Ivan or Leo
   b) Joshua or Leo.

4 When Gary goes to work he is either early, on time or late.
   The probability that he will be on time is 0.16
   The probability that he is early is equal to the probability that he will be late.
   Work out the probability that:
   a) Gary will be late
   b) Gary will be early or on time.

5 There are six pieces of paper in a hat. Each piece of paper has a letter written on it.
The letter is either A or B or C or D or E or F.
A piece of paper is picked at random from the hat.
The table shows the probability that a particular letter will be chosen.

Letter	A	B	C	D	E	F
Probability	0.13	0.02	0.15	0.3	0.24	0.16

Work out the probability that the letter:
a) will not be B
b) will be a vowel.

 EXERCISE 6.2

1 The probability that Brad will be injured in a football match is 0.13
The probability that Marc will be injured in a football match is 0.4
Calculate the probability that:
a) Brad and Marc will both be injured in a football match
b) Brad will be injured and Marc will not be injured in a football match.

2 A fair spinner has four sides numbered 2, 3, 4 and 5
It is spun twice and the numbers are added together.
a) Draw up a two-way table to show the possible combinations of scores.
b) Find the probability that the total score is 8
c) What is the most likely total score?

3 A bag contains 5 blue marbles, 2 red marbles and 6 green marbles.
A marble is chosen at random. It is then replaced, and a second marble is chosen.
a) Work out the probability that the first marble is **not** red.
b) Work out the probability that both marbles are blue.

4 Terri has a three-sided spinner, with the numbers 3, 4 and 5 written on it.
She also has a four-sided spinner, with the numbers 2, 3, 5 and 6 written on it.
Terri spins both spinners and multiplies the two numbers together.
a) Draw up a two-way table to show the possible results.
b) Work out the probability that the product of the two numbers is 15
c) Work out the probability that the product of the two numbers is even.

5 Garth throws a big dice and a small dice.
Both dice are normal fair dice, labelled with the numbers 1, 2, 3, 4, 5, 6
a) Write down the probability that the small dice shows a number bigger than 6
b) Work out the probability that the big dice shows a larger number than the small dice.
c) Work out the probability that Garth throws two even numbers.

6 A box contains coloured pencils which are red or blue or pink.
Jilly takes a pencil from the box at random and puts it back.
The probability that the pencil is red is 0.6
The probability that it is pink is 0.1
a) Write down the probability that Jilly takes a blue pencil.

Ian takes two pencils from the box and puts them back.
b) Work out the probability that Ian takes two red pencils.

Benji takes three pencils from the box.
c) Work out the probability that the first two pencils are the same colour but the third
one is not.

7 In a large box of light bulbs, $\frac{1}{20}$ are defective.
The manager of the store takes two light bulbs from the box.
a) Calculate the probability that the first light bulb is defective and the second one is
not.
b) Calculate the probability that they are both defective.
Give your answers as exact fractions.

8 Each school day Mrs Kothare selects one girl and one boy at random, from some
classes, to show her their homework diaries.
The table shows the probabilities of each student being chosen.

Girls	Year 7	Year 8	Year 9	Year 10
Probability	0.3	0.16	0.42	0.12

Boys	Year 7	Year 8	Year 9	Year 10
Probability	0.2	0.29	0.21	0.3

a) Calculate the probability that Mrs Kothare chooses a girl from Year 9 and a boy from
Year 10
b) Calculate the probability that she chooses a girl and boy from Year 10
There are 200 school days one year.
c) Estimate the number of days Mrs Kothare chooses two Year 7 students.

EXERCISE 6.3

1 Patrick goes for two job interviews. The probability he will be offered the first job is 0.3 and the probability he will be offered the second job is 0.12

   a) Copy and complete the tree diagram to show the possible outcomes of Patrick's job interviews.

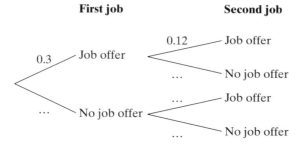

First job   **Second job**

0.12 — Job offer

0.3 — Job offer

... — No job offer

... — Job offer

... — No job offer

... — No job offer

   b) Work out the probability that Patrick is offered both jobs.

   c) Work out the probability that Patrick is offered only one job.

2 Sabia drives to work each morning.
She passes two sets of traffic lights on the way to work.
The probability that a set of traffic lights is green is $\frac{3}{5}$

   a) Draw a tree diagram to represent the possible outcomes of the two traffic lights.

   b) Work out the probability that both sets of traffic lights are green.

   c) Work out the probability that the first set of traffic lights is **not** green and the second set of traffic lights is green.

   d) Work out the probability that just one of the two sets of traffic lights is green.

3 Jean sells two pairs of glasses.
The glasses have either single vision lenses, bifocal lenses or varifocal lenses.
The probability that Jean will sell glasses with single vision lenses is 0.4
The probability that Jean will sell glasses with bifocal lenses is 0.35

   a) Copy and complete the tree diagram.

   b) Find the probability that Jean sells one pair of glasses with bifocal lenses and one pair with varifocal lenses.

   c) Find the probability that Jean does **not** sell two pairs of single vision lenses.

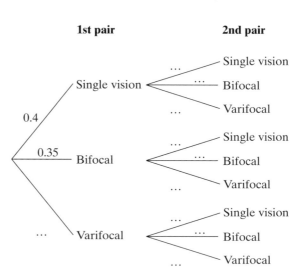

1st pair   **2nd pair**

Single vision
... — Single vision
... — Bifocal
... — Varifocal

0.4

0.35 — Bifocal
... — Single vision
... — Bifocal
... — Varifocal

... — Varifocal
... — Single vision
... — Bifocal
... — Varifocal

4 Jodi has 30 DVDs, 6 of which are musicals.
Wayne has 40 DVDs, 5 of which are musicals.
Jodi and Wayne choose one DVD each at random from their own collections.
  a) Write down the probability that Jodi chooses a musical.
  b) Write down the probability that Wayne chooses a musical.
  c) Draw a tree diagram to illustrate their choices.
  d) Hence find the probability that at least one of them does **not** choose a musical.

5 Louis is a fantastic golfer.
The probability that he gets a hole-in-one (the ball in the hole with one hit) is 0.2
Louis plays three holes at golf.
  a) Illustrate the possible results of getting a hole-in-one, or not, on a tree diagram.
  b) Work out the probability that he gets three holes-in-one.
  c) Work out the probability that he gets exactly one hole-in-one.

6 Deborah (D) and Toby (T) play two games of Snakes and Ladders.
The probability that Deborah will win the first game is 0.1
The probability that she will win the second game is 0.4
  a) Copy and complete the tree diagram.

First game	Second game

```
                              ...        D wins
             ...    D wins  <
     ...   <                  ...        T wins
           <
             ...    T wins  <  ...        D wins
                              ...        T wins
```

  b) Calculate the probability that:
    (i) Deborah will win both games
    (ii) they will each win one game.

EXERCISE 6.4

1 A drawer contains 12 socks. 3 of the socks are red and the rest are black.
Ali is going to take two socks at random from the drawer, **without** replacement.

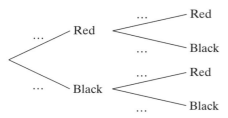

```
                    ...      Red
        ...   Red  <
     <              ...      Black
        ...   Black <  ...   Red
                    ...      Black
```

  a) Copy and complete the tree diagram.
  b) Work out the probability that Ali will take two red socks.
  c) Work out the probability that Ali will take two socks of the same colour.

2 In a class of 30 students, 9 wear glasses and 21 do not wear glasses.
Two students are chosen at random.
  a) Illustrate the situation with a tree diagram.
  b) Calculate the probability that both students wear glasses.
  c) Calculate the probability that at least one student wears glasses.

3 A small box contains 21 chocolates.
15 are milk chocolates and the rest are plain chocolates.
Two chocolates are picked at random, without replacement.
  a) Draw a tree diagram to show this information.
  b) Calculate the probability that one milk chocolate and one plain chocolate are picked.

4 Tanya forecasts the results of 3 tennis matches.
Work out the probability that she forecasts the correct result in all 3 matches.

5 A box contains 25 smarties. 8 are red, 6 are yellow and the rest are green.
Two smarties are chosen at random, without replacement.
  a) Draw a tree diagram to show this information.
  b) Calculate the probability that the two smarties are **not** the same colour.

6 In a bowl of fruit there are 3 bananas, 4 oranges and 5 apples.
Two pieces of fruit are picked at random from the bowl.
  a) Draw a tree diagram to show this information.
  b) Find the probability that 2 oranges are picked.
  c) Work out the probability that two **different** pieces of fruit are picked.

7 There are 15 students in a class.
9 of the students are right-handed, and the other 6 are left-handed.
  a) Two of the 15 students are chosen at random.
    Find the probability that they are both right-handed.
  b) Three of the 15 students are chosen at random.
    Find the probability that they are all left-handed.

UNIT 2

U2 CHAPTER 1

Number

The Exercises in this Chapter are all Stage 1 and Stage 2.

 EXERCISE 1.1

1 Write these numbers in words:
  a) 329   **b)** 1632   **c)** 4 836 007   **d)** 700 508

2 Write these numbers in figures:
  a) three thousand, five hundred and twenty
  b) seven hundred and four
  c) nine and a half thousand
  d) one million, eight hundred and two thousand
  e) five hundred thousand, four hundred and nine
  f) twenty-three thousand, seven hundred and eleven

3 Write these numbers in order of size – start with the smallest number:
  a) 507, 570, 499, 58, 432
  b) 830, 803, 847, 874, 809
  c) 4728, 4900, 4782, 4280, 4903
  d) 23 927, 72 990, 20 999, 9965, 21 973
  e) 1 759 400, 1 489 630, 1 081 927, 2 000 913, 1 050 559
  f) 652 000, 613 028, 607 956, 613 110, 608 280

 EXERCISE 1.2 **2**

1 Work out:
  a) 53 + 61   **b)** 508 + 371   **c)** 79 + 12
  d) 735 + 86   **e)** 612 + 19 + 173   **f)** 908 + 404 + 37

2 Jean went shopping for a fruit salad.
   She wrote a list of what she had bought.

   Work out the total cost of the fruit she bought.

Fruit bought	
Oranges	£2.89
Apples	£1.70
Bananas	63p
Pears	87p
Grapes	£3.05

3 Find the sum of the numbers 6 to 11

4 Add 1209 to 653

5 Increase 258 by 674

6 Mrs Daurat has five children. Their ages are:

Peter	46
Lian	27
David	32
Steve	43
Ben	29

Work out the total age of her children.

7 These pairs of numbers add up to 100
Find the missing value in each pair.
a) 34 and ?
b) 61 and ?
c) 55 and ?
d) 11 and ?
e) 76 and ?
f) 28 and ?

EXERCISE 1.3 ① ②

1 Work out:
a) $87 - 45$
b) $623 - 411$
c) $56 - 39$
d) $725 - 58$
e) $812 - 375$
f) $1467 - 889$

2 Decrease 719 by 304   3 Subtract 279 from 813

4 What number needs to be added to 38 to make 100?

5 Four students sat a Mathematics examination.
The table shows their total marks out of 300:

Graham	213
Keith	95
Julie	187
Uzma	261

a) What is the difference between Graham's and Keith's marks?
b) How many more marks did Uzma get than Graham?
c) What is the difference between Julie's mark and Uzma's mark?
d) What is the difference between the highest mark and the lowest mark?
e) How many marks did the four students get in total?

EXERCISE 1.4 ① ②

1 Copy and complete this times table grid:

×	1	3	4	6	8	9	10
1	1			6			
2			8			18	
4		12					
5	5					45	
7			28				
8	8						
9		27					90

2 Work out:
a) 5×8
b) 9×3
c) 4×7
d) 6×2
e) 5×7
f) 8×6
g) 10×9
h) 7×6
i) $5 \times 2 \times 7$
j) $4 \times 5 \times 6$
k) $3 \times 2 \times 9$
l) $1 \times 1 \times 8$

3 Find the missing values:
a) $7 \times ? = 42$
b) $6 \times ? = 48$
c) $? \times 10 = 70$
d) $? \times 5 = 45$
e) $3 \times ? = 27$
f) $? \times 4 = 20$
g) $9 \times ? = 18$
h) $1 \times ? = 1$
i) $3 \times 2 \times ? = 30$
j) $? \times 4 \times 2 = 64$

EXERCISE 1.5

1 Multiply the following numbers by 10:
- **a)** 8
- **b)** 57
- **c)** 60
- **d)** 914
- **e)** 2.36
- **f)** 7.7
- **g)** 0.8
- **h)** 0.45

2 Multiply the following numbers by 100:
- **a)** 4
- **b)** 23
- **c)** 86
- **d)** 308
- **e)** 0.5
- **f)** 5.36
- **g)** 1.7
- **h)** 0.09

3 Multiply the following numbers by 1000:
- **a)** 5
- **b)** 90
- **c)** 436
- **d)** 807
- **e)** 1.936
- **f)** 0.064
- **g)** 0.51
- **h)** 23.7

4 Work out:
- **a)** 6×30
- **b)** 8×20
- **c)** 5×70
- **d)** 4×900
- **e)** 3×600
- **f)** 7×200
- **g)** 30×50
- **h)** 800×40
- **i)** 70×20
- **j)** 2×800
- **k)** 50×60
- **l)** 700×3

EXERCISE 1.6 1 2

1 Divide the following numbers by 10:
- **a)** 70
- **b)** 630
- **c)** 4500
- **d)** 30 000
- **e)** 57
- **f)** 91
- **g)** 6.2
- **h)** 0.46

2 Divide the following numbers by 100:
- **a)** 7000
- **b)** 300
- **c)** 58 700
- **d)** 2 670 000
- **e)** 19
- **f)** 47
- **g)** 0.58
- **h)** 9.123

3 Divide the following numbers by 1000:
- **a)** 2000
- **b)** 245 000
- **c)** 63 000
- **d)** 3 700 000
- **e)** 900
- **f)** 60
- **g)** 81
- **h)** 5.4

4 Work out:
- **a)** $4000 \div 50$
- **b)** $420 \div 70$
- **c)** $3500 \div 700$
- **d)** $28 000 \div 400$
- **e)** $3500 \div 50$
- **f)** $48 000 \div 600$
- **g)** $600 \div 20$
- **h)** $6300 \div 900$
- **i)** $240 000 \div 3000$
- **j)** $56 000 \div 80$

EXERCISE 1.7 1 2

1 Work out:
- **a)** 15×26
- **b)** 37×54
- **c)** 29×17
- **d)** 163×23
- **e)** 191×32
- **f)** 271×59
- **g)** 135×16
- **h)** 284×43
- **i)** 167×84

2 A large company posted 174 parcels. Each parcel needed an 83p stamp. Work out the total cost of the stamps.

3 There are 23 biscuits in each packet of Eatsumore biscuits.
- **a)** Work out how many biscuits there are in 54 packets.

Each packet of biscuits costs £1.36
- **b)** Work out the total cost of the 54 packets.

EXERCISE 1.8 **1** **2**

1 Work out:
  a) $315 \div 5$ **b)** $432 \div 8$ **c)** $282 \div 6$
  d) $882 \div 14$ **e)** $221 \div 17$ **f)** $377 \div 13$
  g) $522 \div 29$ **h)** $966 \div 42$ **i)** $952 \div 56$

2 Work out the following and write down the remainder in each question:
  a) $68 \div 7$ **b)** $45 \div 4$ **c)** $614 \div 17$
  d) $463 \div 25$ **e)** $379 \div 11$ **f)** $381 \div 12$

3 A box can hold 18 books.
  Work out how many boxes will be needed to hold 666 books.

4 A librarian has £489 to spend on dictionaries.
  Each dictionary costs £23
  How many dictionaries can the librarian buy?

 EXERCISE 1.9 **1** **2**

1 Ahmed went to a cafe.
  He ordered:
    3 sausages
    2 fried eggs
    baked beans
    mushrooms
  He paid with a £5 note.
  Work out how much change he got.

MENU	
Sausages	42p each
Fishcakes	87p each
Fried eggs	35p each
Onions	28p
Mushrooms	47p
Baked beans	50p

2 Mrs Fox buys rulers for her class.
  Each ruler costs 17p
  How many rulers can Mrs Fox buy if she has £5.00?

3 A florist sells roses at 36p each.
  Nina buys 144 roses for a function.
  Work out the total cost of the 144 roses.

4 Mary is 153 cm tall and weighs 104 kg
  John is 23 cm taller than Mary but weighs 17 kg less than her.
  Work out John's height and weight.

5 Boris plants bulbs along the border of his garden.
  He plants the bulbs 23 cm apart.
  If the length of the border is 675 cm, work out how many bulbs he planted.

6 Sunita buys 27 postcards. Each postcard costs 16p
  How much change will Sunita get if she pays with a £10 note?

EXERCISE 1.10

Do not use your calculator for Questions 1–5.

1 Work out:
a) $5 + 7$
b) $-2 + 8$
c) $-7 + 4$
d) $-3 + 9$
e) $1 + -3$
f) $-7 + -2$

2 Work out:
a) $9 - 5$
b) $-8 - 1$
c) $-7 - 3$
d) $7 - -2$
e) $6 - -3$
f) $-5 - -2$

3 Work out:
a) $6 + -3$
b) $-5 - -1$
c) $-8 + -3$
d) $-2 - 7$
e) $-9 - -9$
f) $-4 + -3$

4 Write these numbers in order of size. Write the smallest number first.
a) $-5, \ 7, \ 3, \ -4, \ -1, \ 4$
b) $8, \ -6, \ -7, \ 6, \ 0, \ -2$
c) $-3, \ 5, \ -9, \ -4, \ 7, \ 3$
d) $1, \ 0, \ -1, \ -5, \ 3, \ -2$

5 On 1st January at noon the temperature in six cities was recorded.
a) Write down:
(i) the highest temperature
(ii) the lowest temperature.
b) Work out the difference in temperature between Moscow and New York.
c) Work out the difference in temperature between London and New York.

The temperature in Oslo was 12 °C lower than in Barcelona.

d) Write down the temperature in Oslo.

City	Temperature (°C)
Moscow	−23
London	3
Cape Town	21
New York	−4
Barcelona	7

You can use your calculator for Questions 6 and 7.

6 Six people were in a competition. Each round they were awarded plus (+) points if they did well and minus (−) points if they did badly. The table gives information about their points.

Copy and complete the table.

Competitor	Round 1	Round 2	Total
Andy	+23	−20	
Brian	+4	−7	
Carol	−6		−10
Deborah	−3		+4
Ed		+5	−1
Frances		−9	+8

7 Gary has £5 and earns £26
He owes his mum £32 and his dad £19
He buys some food for £8 and gives £3 to charity.
His grandmother gives him £50 for his birthday.
Work out how much money Gary will have left if he pays all his debts.

EXERCISE 1.11

Work out the following:

1 5×-4	**2** -3×-10	**3** -7×3
4 $-45 \div -9$	**5** $70 \div -7$	**6** 8×-2
7 $-36 \div -4$	**8** -4×-4	**9** $-18 \div 6$
10 6×-7	**11** -8×-5	**12** 11×-6
13 $48 \div -6$	**14** $35 \div -7$	**15** 5×-9

Be careful not to mix up all the different rules you have learnt.
Work out:

16 $-81 \div 9$	**17** $-3 + -7$	**18** $-6 - -8$
19 $-24 \div -6$	**20** 7×-8	**21** $-63 \div 9$
22 $-6 - -3$	**23** $-1 + -7$	**24** $7 + -9$
25 -6×3	**26** $8 \div -2$	**27** $6 + -6$

EXERCISE 1.12

1 Round these numbers to the nearest 10:   **a)** 23   **b)** 151   **c)** 867   **d)** 405

2 Round these numbers to the nearest 100:   **a)** 382   **b)** 849   **c)** 550   **d)** 6351

3 Round these numbers to the nearest 1000:   **a)** 676   **b)** 8099   **c)** 549   **d)** 3520

4 Round these numbers to the nearest integer: **a)** 6.7   **b)** 23.4   **c)** 9.2   **d)** 5.813

5 Round these numbers to 1 significant figure:
   a) 28   **b)** 73   **c)** 267   **d)** 155
   e) 3792   **f)** 408   **g)** 6193   **h)** 8705

6 Round these numbers to 2 significant figures:
   a) 813   **b)** 506   **c)** 127   **d)** 981
   e) 6352   **f)** 4438   **g)** 1823   **h)** 7907

EXERCISE 1.13

1 By rounding to 1 significant figure, work out an approximate answer to:
   a) 213×57 **b)** $738 - 497$ **c)** $897 \div 305$

   d) $\dfrac{63 \times 27}{85}$ **e)** $\dfrac{815 \times 28}{782 - 213}$ **f)** $\dfrac{91 \times 387}{903 - 285}$

   g) $\dfrac{7.6 \times 2.81}{3.19 + 2.73}$ **h)** $\dfrac{7.2(3.06 + 1.15)}{1.93 \times 6.8}$ **i)** $\dfrac{5.95(9.93 - 4.17)}{8.05 - 3.72}$

2 A large box contains 189 books each costing £3.28
   a) Estimate the total paid for the box of books.
   A school orders 5 of these boxes of books.
   b) Estimate the total cost of all 5 boxes of books.

U2 CHAPTER 2

Decimals

The Exercises in this Chapter are all Stage 1 and Stage 2.

 EXERCISE 1.1

1 Round these numbers to 1 decimal place:
- **a)** 5.26
- **b)** 2.849
- **c)** 3.28
- **d)** 12.438
- **e)** 7.081
- **f)** 23.127
- **g)** 19.45
- **h)** 10.792

2 Round these numbers to 2 decimal places:
- **a)** 3.333
- **b)** 8.279
- **c)** 6.544
- **d)** 16.826
- **e)** 7.007
- **f)** 4.3571
- **g)** 8.996
- **h)** 11.9519

3 Round 16.708 352 to:
- **a)** 1 decimal place
- **b)** 2 decimal places
- **c)** 3 decimal places
- **d)** 4 decimal places.

 EXERCISE 2.2

1 Work out:
- **a)** 0.4 + 0.5 + 0.3
- **b)** 0.6 + 0.1
- **c)** 2.2 + 3.1 + 0.8
- **d)** 5.23 + 8.19
- **e)** 8.03 + 2.91
- **f)** 7.54 + 6.13

2 Work out:
- **a)** 2.54 + 0.2
- **b)** 9.1 + 6.62
- **c)** 5.283 + 2.15
- **d)** 14.38 + 2.7
- **e)** 19.03 + 4.235
- **f)** 8.29 + 3.6 + 1.03

3 Work out:
- **a)** 5.3 − 2.1
- **b)** 0.85 − 0.24
- **c)** 9.37 − 4.17
- **d)** 12.7 − 3.9
- **e)** 24.61 − 20.24
- **f)** 37.73 − 14.61 − 3.01

4 Work out:
- **a)** 19.23 − 14.7
- **b)** 7.37 − 2.1
- **c)** 54.17 − 27.1
- **d)** 0.835 − 0.64
- **e)** 7.8 − 2.39
- **f)** 37.2 − 25.56

 EXERCISE 2.3

1 Work out:
- **a)** 7 × 0.2
- **b)** 0.5 × 9
- **c)** 0.1 × 8
- **d)** 4 × 0.6
- **e)** 5 × 0.3
- **f)** 0.7 × 3
- **g)** 0.9 × 4
- **h)** 2 × 0.1
- **i)** 12 × 0.1

2 Work out:
- **a)** 0.5 × 0.3
- **b)** 0.8 × 0.1
- **c)** 0.05 × 0.6
- **d)** 0.09 × 0.02
- **e)** 0.04 × 0.07
- **f)** 1.2 × 0.3
- **g)** 6.27 × 0.3
- **h)** 5.09 × 0.2
- **i)** 2.8 × 3.6

3 Work out:
a) 5.7×1.4 b) 7.14×3.8 c) 6.71×9.2
d) 2.3×4.17 e) 6.53×2.8 f) 5.79×3
g) 8.04×3.6 h) $0.2 \times 0.3 \times 0.5$ i) $2.1 \times 0.1 \times 0.3$

4 Use the fact that $215 \times 38 = 8170$ to work out:
a) 2.15×3.8 b) 21.5×0.38 c) 215×3.8 d) 0.215×38

5 Use the fact that $518 \times 74 = 38\,332$ to work out:
a) 51.8×7.4 b) 518×0.74 c) 5.18×7.4 d) 0.518×7.4

 EXERCISE 2.4

1 Work out:
a) $9 \div 0.3$ b) $8 \div 0.4$ c) $7 \div 0.1$
d) $24 \div 0.08$ e) $35 \div 0.05$ f) $28 \div 0.07$
g) $42 \div 0.06$ h) $100 \div 0.04$ i) $25 \div 0.5$

2 Work out:
a) $3.6 \div 0.3$ b) $0.4 \div 0.2$ c) $0.15 \div 0.3$
d) $5.4 \div 0.09$ e) $0.64 \div 0.08$ f) $2.5 \div 0.5$
g) $0.49 \div 0.07$ h) $6.3 \div 0.09$ i) $81.9 \div 0.3$

3 Use the fact that $306 \div 17 = 18$ to work out:
a) $30.6 \div 17$ b) $306 \div 0.17$ c) $3.06 \div 1.7$ d) $0.306 \div 0.17$

4 Use the fact that $28 \times 64 = 1792$ to work out:
a) (i) $1792 \div 64$ (ii) $179.2 \div 28$ (iii) $17.92 \div 2.8$
b) (i) $1.792 \div 0.28$ (ii) $17.92 \div 0.64$ (iii) $1792 \div 6.4$

 EXERCISE 2.5

1 What numbers are the arrows **a**, **b**, **c** and **d** pointing to?

2 What numbers are the arrows **a**, **b**, **c** and **d** pointing to?

3 a) Write down the number marked with an arrow.

b) Write down the number marked with an arrow.

c) Find the number 620 on the number line. On a copy, mark it with an arrow (↑).

d) Find the number 4.9 on the number line. On a copy, mark it with an arrow (↑).

4 a) Write down the number marked with an arrow.

b) Write down the number marked with an arrow.

c) Find the number 57 on the number line. On a copy, mark it with an arrow (↑).

d) Find the number 3.9 on the number line. On a copy, mark it with an arrow (↑).

EXERCISE 2.6 ❶ ❷

Do not use your calculator for Questions 1–5.

1 Daniel buys 4 cans of cola at 82p each.
  a) How much does he spend?
  b) How much change does he get from £5?

2 A CD costs £7.50
   Work out the cost of 9 of these CDs.

3 Gary is taking his family to the zoo.
Gary buys zoo tickets for 2 adults and 5 children.
  a) How much does he spend on tickets?

Gary buys 7 sandwiches, 3 fruit juices and 5 chocolates.

Sandwiches	£2.20
Fruit juice	£1.34
Chocolates	£0.57

ZOO	
Adults	£9.30
Children	£6.00

  b) How much does Gary spend on food and drinks?
  c) How much does the zoo trip cost altogether?

4 Sunita orders soup, a burger and an ice cream.
Work out how much change she should get from £4

Menu	
Soup	86p
Burger	£1.64
Ice cream	60p

5 Will has twenty pounds and thirty-eight pence.
  a) Write down the amount of money Will has in figures.
Will spends £8.53
  b) How much money does he have left?

You may use your calculator for Questions 6–8.

6 Mia travels 100 km in a Haver taxi.
  a) Work out the total amount she has to pay.

Fred travels in a Haver taxi. He pays £68
  b) How far did Fred travel in the Haver taxi?

Haver Taxis Charges
£35.20 for the first 50 km
£4.10 for each 10 km after this

7 Suzy hires a car. She pays:
       £43.80 for the first day and
       £32.50 for each extra day.
Suzy hires a car for 1 week.
  a) How much does she pay?

Kevin pays £433.80 to hire a car.
  b) For how many days does he hire a car?

8 Jean went to the supermarket. She bought:
       2 cartons of soup at £1.12 per carton
       $1\frac{1}{2}$ kg of salmon at £14.10 per kg
       4 kg potatoes at £1.07 per kg
       3 melons at £2.16 each.

Work out how much change Jean should get from £40

U2 CHAPTER 3

Fractions and percentages

Exercises 3.1, 3.2, 3.3 and 3.4 are Stage 1. All Exercises are Stage 2.

 EXERCISE 3.1

1 Write the following fractions as decimals:

a) $\frac{1}{4}$ **b)** $\frac{3}{8}$ **c)** $\frac{2}{5}$ **d)** $\frac{1}{3}$ **e)** $\frac{9}{100}$ **f)** $\frac{13}{20}$ **g)** $\frac{5}{6}$ **h)** $\frac{7}{12}$

2 Write the following numbers in order of size from smallest to biggest:

a) $\frac{2}{3}$, 0.61, $\frac{3}{5}$, 0.67, 0.605   **b)** 0.22, $\frac{1}{5}$, $\frac{1}{6}$, 0.18, $\frac{2}{7}$

c) $\frac{17}{20}$, 0.83, 0.819, $\frac{4}{5}$, 0.851   **d)** 0.38, $\frac{4}{11}$, 0.4, 0.3, $\frac{1}{3}$

 Do not use your calculator for Question 3.

3 Write the following fractions as decimals:

a) $\frac{3}{10}$ **b)** $\frac{11}{25}$ **c)** $\frac{4}{5}$ **d)** $\frac{79}{100}$ **e)** $\frac{9}{20}$

f) $\frac{3}{4}$ **g)** $\frac{7}{8}$ **h)** $\frac{7}{100}$ **i)** $\frac{3}{20}$

 EXERCISE 3.2

1 Match together equivalent fractions. $\boxed{\frac{20}{32}}$ $\boxed{\frac{2}{9}}$ $\boxed{\frac{5}{8}}$

Do not use your calculator for Questions 2 to 6.

2 Write these fractions in their simplest form:

a) $\frac{24}{72}$ **b)** $\frac{42}{84}$ **c)** $\frac{8}{20}$ **d)** $\frac{5}{35}$ **e)** $\frac{9}{27}$ **f)** $\frac{50}{175}$ **g)** $\frac{72}{96}$ **h)** $\frac{39}{45}$

3 Find the missing values in these equivalent fractions:

a) $\frac{1}{5} = \frac{?}{10} = \frac{3}{?} = \frac{?}{25} = \frac{?}{55}$ **b)** $\frac{3}{4} = \frac{9}{?} = \frac{12}{?} = \frac{?}{40} = \frac{?}{60}$

c) $\frac{2}{3} = \frac{8}{?} = \frac{?}{24} = \frac{24}{?} = \frac{?}{60}$ **d)** $\frac{7}{10} = \frac{?}{20} = \frac{?}{30} = \frac{49}{?} = \frac{77}{?}$

4 Write these fractions in order of size:

a) $\frac{3}{4}$, $\frac{5}{8}$, $\frac{7}{16}$ **b)** $\frac{2}{5}$, $\frac{7}{20}$, $\frac{3}{10}$ **c)** $\frac{1}{4}$, $\frac{1}{6}$, $\frac{1}{3}$, $\frac{3}{24}$, $\frac{3}{8}$

d) $\frac{1}{2}$, $\frac{2}{3}$, $\frac{3}{5}$, $\frac{7}{10}$, $\frac{17}{30}$ **e)** $\frac{2}{3}$, $\frac{3}{4}$, $\frac{3}{6}$, $\frac{5}{12}$ **f)** $\frac{3}{10}$, $\frac{31}{100}$, $\frac{297}{1000}$

5 Write the following as mixed numbers:

a) $\frac{9}{5}$ **b)** $\frac{11}{3}$ **c)** $\frac{5}{2}$ **d)** $\frac{7}{4}$ **e)** $\frac{13}{5}$ **f)** $\frac{22}{7}$

6 Write the following as top-heavy fractions:

   a) $1\frac{3}{5}$ **b)** $2\frac{1}{4}$ **c)** $1\frac{5}{7}$ **d)** $4\frac{2}{3}$ **e)** $5\frac{1}{6}$ **f)** $3\frac{1}{3}$ **g)** $6\frac{1}{2}$ **h)** $2\frac{4}{9}$

EXERCISE 3.3 ❶ ❷

Write the following decimals as fractions in their simplest form:

1 0.1   **2** 0.3   **3** 0.25   **4** 0.125   **5** 0.86

6 0.44   **7** 0.325   **8** 0.92   **9** 0.06

EXERCISE 3.4 ❶ ❷

Do not use your calculator for Questions 1–5.

1 Change these percentages to decimals:

   a) 52% **b)** 38% **c)** 91% **d)** 3%   **e)** 7%   **f)** 6.2% **g)** 0.4% **h)** 205%

2 Change these decimals to percentages:

   a) 0.37 **b)** 0.58 **c)** 0.6   **d)** 0.09 **e)** 0.04 **f)** 0.1   **g)** 3.85 **h)** 9.2

3 Change these fractions to percentages:

   a) $\frac{63}{100}$ **b)** $\frac{17}{100}$ **c)** $\frac{5}{100}$ **d)** $\frac{27}{50}$ **e)** $\frac{3}{10}$ **f)** $\frac{2}{5}$ **g)** $\frac{17}{25}$ **h)** $\frac{3}{4}$

4 Change these percentages to fractions. Write each answer in its simplest form.

   a) 65% **b)** 90% **c)** 36% **d)** 4%   **e)** 12% **f)** 340% **g)** 12.5% **h)** 50%

5 Change these fractions to decimals:

   a) $\frac{1}{2}$ **b)** $\frac{1}{5}$ **c)** $\frac{3}{10}$ **d)** $\frac{9}{100}$ **e)** $\frac{23}{100}$ **f)** $\frac{3}{50}$ **g)** $\frac{3}{4}$ **h)** $\frac{11}{25}$

You can use your calculator for Questions 6 and 7.

6 Change these fractions to percentages:

   a) $\frac{28}{50}$ **b)** $\frac{15}{20}$ **c)** $\frac{57}{60}$ **d)** $\frac{12}{30}$ **e)** $\frac{24}{60}$ **f)** $\frac{22}{55}$ **g)** $\frac{12}{40}$ **h)** $\frac{36}{80}$

7 Copy and complete the following table.

Percentage	Decimal	Fraction
	0.25	
		$\frac{1}{2}$
10%		
	0.3333	$\frac{1}{3}$
	0.9	
$66\frac{2}{3}$%		
		$\frac{3}{4}$
80%		
	0.05	
20%		

 EXERCISE 3.5

1 Work out:
 a) 30% of 360 **b)** 20% of 45 **c)** 80% of 65 **d)** 7% of 300
 e) 25% of 420 **f)** 42% of 60 **g)** 10% of 810 **h)** 2% of 790
 i) 2.5% of 400 **j)** 17.5% of 1000 **k)** 150% of 6342 **l)** 130% of 500

2 Jon buys a video recorder.
How much VAT does he pay?

> **SPECIAL OFFER!**
> *Video Recorder*
> only £290 plus 17.5% VAT

3 In a Mathematics test 84% of the students passed.
 a) What percentage of the students did not pass?

200 students sat the test.
 b) How many students passed the test?

4

> **STEVE'S SAUSAGES**
> 72% beef

> **BERTIE'S BANGERS**
> 44 g out of every 60 g beef

Rob wants to buy the sausages that contain the most beef.
Which sausages should he buy? Explain why.

5 Neil gets 2% commission for every house he sells.
Work out how much commission he gets when he sells houses for:
 a) £320 000 **b)** £65 500 **c)** £1 270 000

EXERCISE 3.6 **2**

1 Find **(i)** 10% **(ii)** 5% **(iii)** 15% of:
   a) 300   **b)** 40   **c)** 1500   **d)** 76

2 Find 25% of:
   a) 300   **b)** 20   **c)** 6400   **d)** 48

3 Find:
   a) 50% of 146   **b)** 25% of 280   **c)** 5% of 60
   d) 7.5% of 200   **e)** 10% of 6530   **f)** 40% of 55
   g) 20% of 350   **h)** 65% of 2400   **i)** 70% of 700

4 Work out the VAT (at 17.5%) that needs to be paid on the following items.
   a)   **b)**   **c)**

   | TV set | Oil painting | Electronic organiser |
   | price: £250 | price: £6200 | price: £180 |

5 A shop offers a discount of 15% to all of its customers.
   How much is the discount on the following items?
   a)   **b)**   **c)**

   | Gold earrings | Silver clock | Gold pen |
   | price: £320 | price: £680 | price: £84 |

6 a) Find 10% of £600
   b) Find 10% of your answer to **a)**.
   c) State which of these amounts is the same as your answer to **b)**:
          1% of £600   or   20% of £600

7 a) Find 20% of £90
   b) Find 50% of your answer to **a)**.
   c) State which of these amounts is the same as your answer to **b)**:
          10% of £90   or   70% of £90

U2 CHAPTER 4

Powers and roots

Exercises 4.1, 4.7 and 4.8 are Stage 1. Exercises 4.2, 4.3, 4.4, 4.5, 4.6, 4.8 and 4.9 are Stage 2.

EXERCISE 4.1 ①

1 a) Write down the first six multiples of:
  (i) 9   **(ii)** 12   **(iii)** 18   **(iv)** 24   **(v)** 36

  b) Find the **least common multiple** of:
  (i) 12 and 18   **(ii)** 9 and 24   **(iii)** 18 and 24   **(iv)** 24 and 36

2 a) Find the factors of:
  (i) 15   **(ii)** 18   **(iii)** 24   **(iv)** 120

  b) Find the **highest common factor** of:
  (i) 15 and 18   **(ii)** 18 and 24   **(iii)** 18 and 120

3 Which of the following numbers are **not** prime? Give a reason for each answer.

  $\quad$ 15 $\quad$ 17 $\quad$ 26 $\quad$ 31 $\quad$ 35 $\quad$ 49 $\quad$ 53 $\quad$ 60 $\quad$ 67

4 a) Which of the following numbers are prime?
  If it is not prime, give a number that goes into it exactly.
  7, 17, 27, 37, 47, 57, 67, 77, 87, 97

  b) Which of the following numbers are prime?
  If it is not prime, give a number that goes into it exactly.
  9, 19, 29, 39, 49, 59, 69, 79, 89, 99

EXERCISE 4.2 ②

1 Square the following numbers:
  a) 4   **b)** 7   **c)** 8   **d)** 10   **e)** 11

2 Work out:
  a) 3^2 **b)** 5^2 **c)** 8^2 **d)** 6^2 **e)** 12^2

3 Write down the first 10 square numbers.

4 Work out: **a)** $\sqrt{16}$ **b)** $\sqrt{25}$ **c)** $\sqrt{49}$ **d)** $\sqrt{1}$

5 2500 counters are arranged in a square.
  How many counters are along one side of the square?

6 a) (i) Square root 16 and then square your answer.
  (ii) Square root 36 and then square your answer.
  (iii) What do you notice?

  b) Work out: **(i)** $(\sqrt{7})^2$ **(ii)** $(\sqrt{11})^2$ **(iii)** $(\sqrt{20})^2$

7 Write down the whole number that is closest in value to:
  a) $\sqrt{24}$ **b)** $\sqrt{6}$ **c)** $\sqrt{97}$ **d)** $\sqrt{11}$

8 Estimate: **a)** $\sqrt{50}$ **b)** $\sqrt{108}$ **c)** $\sqrt{28}$ **d)** $\sqrt{5}$

9 Find the square root of: **a)** 36   **b)** 81   **c)** 64   **d)** 100

EXERCISE 4.3 ②

1 Work out:
   a) $\sqrt{361}$ **b)** $\sqrt{39.69}$ **c)** $\sqrt{0.09}$ **d)** $\sqrt{70.56}$

2 Work out the following. Give your answers to 1 decimal place:
   a) 3.6^2 **b)** 9.7^2 **c)** 24.1^2 **d)** 43.3^2

3 Work out the following. Give your answers to 3 significant figures:
   a) $3.8^2 + \sqrt{250}$ **b)** $\sqrt{52} - \sqrt{37}$ **c)** $21.9^2 - \sqrt{126}$

4 Work out the following. Give your answers to 3 significant figures:
   a) $\dfrac{\sqrt{983}}{6.7^2}$ **b)** $\dfrac{4.1^2}{\sqrt{9.2}}$ **c)** $\dfrac{\sqrt{543}}{2.1^2}$

5 Find the square root of:
   a) 1369   **b)** 1.44   **c)** 204.49   **d)** 21.16

EXERCISE 4.4 ②

1 Which of the following numbers are cube numbers?
       4   8   16   27   64

2 Work out:
   a) 1^3 **b)** 6^3 **c)** 10^3 **d)** 0.2^3

3 Work out:
   a) $\sqrt[3]{2744}$ **b)** $\sqrt[3]{125}$ **c)** $\sqrt[3]{0.001}$ **d)** $\sqrt[3]{4.913}$

4 a) Find the cube of   **(i)** 2   **(ii)** 6   **(iii)** 11
   b) Find the cube root of   **(i)** 27   **(ii)** 0.064   **(iii)** 8000

EXERCISE 4.5 ②

1 Write the following using indices:
   a) $2 \times 2 \times 2 \times 2 \times 2 \times 2$ **b)** $5 \times 5 \times 5 \times 5$
   c) $8 \times 8 \times 8 \times 8 \times 8 \times 8 \times 8 \times 8$ **d)** $1 \times 1 \times 1$
   e) $4.7 \times 4.7 \times 4.7 \times 4.7 \times 4.7$ **f)** $9.3 \times 9.3 \times 9.3 \times 9.3 \times 9.3 \times 9.3 \times 9.3$

2 Use your calculator to work out:
   a) 6^4 **b)** 8^3 **c)** 1^{23} **d)** 3^7 **e)** 2^9 **f)** 9^5

3 Use your calculator to work out:
   a) $\sqrt[5]{243}$ **b)** $\sqrt[9]{1}$ **c)** $\sqrt[8]{6561}$ **d)** $\sqrt[5]{32\,768}$ **e)** $\sqrt[4]{0.4096}$ **f)** $\sqrt[7]{128}$

4 a) Match together cards with the same answer.

$3^5 \times 3^3$	$3^6 \div 3^5$	3^3	3^8	$3^7 \times 3^2$	$3^7 \div 3^3$
3^1	3^5	3×3^4	$3^5 \div 3^2$	3^9	3^4

   b) What do you notice?

EXERCISE 4.6 ②

Do not use your calculator for Questions 1 and 2.

1 Write each of the following as a single power:
   a) $7^5 \times 7^9$ **b)** $2^{10} \times 2^6$ **c)** $10^8 \div 10^2$ **d)** $5^{18} \div 5^6$
   e) $8^4 \times 8^5$ **f)** $9^9 \times 9$ **g)** $15^{80} \div 15^{50}$ **h)** $37^{14} \div 37^7$
   i) $2.6^3 \times 2.6^4$ **j)** $58^8 \times 58^8$ **k)** $\dfrac{6^{15}}{6^3}$ **l)** $\dfrac{9^{12}}{9^9}$

2 Write each of the following as a single power:
   a) $\dfrac{7^3 \times 7^8}{7^6}$ **b)** $\dfrac{3^9 \times 3^5}{3^7}$ **c)** $\dfrac{8^2 \times 8^9}{8^4}$

You can use your calculator for Questions 3 and 4.

3 a) Write the following as a single power:
   (i) $\dfrac{5^7}{5^6}$ **(ii)** $\dfrac{8^5}{8^4}$ **(iii)** $\dfrac{6^9}{6^8}$

   b) Work out the value of:
   (i) $\dfrac{5^7}{5^6}$ **(ii)** $\dfrac{8^5}{8^4}$ **(iii)** $\dfrac{6^9}{6^8}$

   c) How else can you write x^1?

4 a) Write the following as a single power:
   (i) $\dfrac{4^7}{4^7}$ **(ii)** $\dfrac{9^8}{9^8}$ **(iii)** $\dfrac{2^{10}}{2^{10}}$

   b) Work out the value of:
   (i) $\dfrac{4^7}{4^7}$ **(ii)** $\dfrac{9^8}{9^8}$ **(iii)** $\dfrac{2^{10}}{2^{10}}$

   c) What does x^0 always equal?

EXERCISE 4.7 ①

1 Write each of the following numbers as a product of prime factors.
   a) 24   **b)** 63   **c)** 45   **d)** 120   **e)** 36
   f) 84   **g)** 30   **h)** 420   **i)** 90

2 Find the **(i)** highest common factor and **(ii)** least common multiple of:
   a) 36 and 45   **b)** 63 and 84   **c)** 90 and 420
   d) 36 and 63   **e)** 120 and 420   **f)** 30 and 45
   g) 84 and 420   **h)** 24 and 90   **i)** 24 and 36

EXERCISE 4.8 ① ②

1 Work out:

   a) $6 + 3 \times 2$ **b)** $10 \div 2 + 3$ **c)** $(7 + 2) \times 2 + 5$

   d) $3 \times 8 - 6 \times 2$ **e)** $\dfrac{9 \times 2}{5 + 1}$ **f)** $\dfrac{5 + 3^2}{2^3 - 1}$

   g) $\dfrac{10 - 4 \times 2}{12 \div 6}$ **h)** $\dfrac{15 - 2 \times 3}{10 - (5 + 4)}$

2 Use your calculator to work out the following.
Give your answers to 1 decimal place:

a) $23 - \sqrt{37}$

b) $7 \times \sqrt{(26 \div 4)}$

c) $\dfrac{15.8 + 3.72}{8.9 - 4.01}$

d) $7.8^2 + 12.3$

e) $93.4 \div (2 + \sqrt{45})$

f) $\dfrac{17^2 - 13^2}{\sqrt{(8.2 - 3.56)}}$

g) $\dfrac{62.1 \times 23.4}{7.8^2 + \sqrt{37}}$

h) $\dfrac{\sqrt{2378}}{9.7^2}$

3 Insert brackets into the following sums to make them correct.
   a) $6 + 9 \div 3 = 5$
   b) $8 \times 6 + 3 \div 6 - 3 = 9$
   c) $2.4 + 7.2 \times 3.7 - 1.6 = 20.16$

EXERCISE 4.9

1 Work out:
   a) 10^3
   b) 10^5
   c) 10^9

2 Write the following as a power of 10:
   a) $10\,000$
   b) $100\,000\,000$
   c) $1\,000\,000\,000\,000$

3 10^{100} is called a 'googol'.
   One hundred googols is written as 1 followed by how many zeros?

4 Write each of the following: **(i)** using powers of 10; **(ii)** as an ordinary number.
   a) 5 hundred thousand
   b) 3 million
   c) 70 thousand

5 Use your calculator to work out the following, giving your answer in standard index form:
   a) $(2.7 \times 10^5) \times (3 \times 10^7)$
   b) $(7.8 \times 10^{15}) \div (2 \times 10^{11})$
   c) $(3.6 \times 10^8) \times (1.9 \times 10^{13})$
   d) $(5.1 \times 10^{23}) \div (3 \times 10^{12})$

U2 CHAPTER 5

Working with algebra

Exercises 5.1, 5.2 and 5.3 are Stage 1. All Exercises are Stage 2.

EXERCISE 5.1

1 Write down expressions for the following:
 a) 3 more than x **b)** 8 more than w
 c) 5 less than v **d)** 23 multiplied by c
 e) r lots of 4   **f)** r squared
 g) $5a$ more than 3b   **h)** 23 divided by d
 i) the sum of g and $2h$ **j)** p divided by q
 k) $3e$ all squared   **l)** t divided by u
 m) 5 lots of f squared   **n)** c squared multiplied by n cubed

2 Kevin has k sweets.
 Julie has 5 more sweets than Kevin.
 a) Write down an expression, in terms of k, for the number of sweets that Julie has.
 Peter has 8 more sweets than Julie.
 b) Write down an expression, in terms of k, for the number of sweets that Peter has.
 Joe has 3 times as many sweets as Peter.
 c) Write down an expression, in terms of k, for the number of sweets that Joe has.
 d) Kevin has 17 sweets. How many sweets does Joe have?

3 The base of a parallelogram is 7 cm more than its height, h
 a) Write down an expression, in terms of h, for
 the base of the parallelogram.
 b) Write down an expression, in terms of h, for
 the area of the parallelogram.
 c) Work out the area of parallelogram when:
 (i) $h = 5$ cm   **(ii)** $h = 1$ cm   **(iii)** $h = 4$ cm

Remember that the
area of a parallelogram
is base × height

4 Write down an expression for the
 area of this square. x cm
 a) Nine of these squares are put
 together to make a large square:
 b) Write down an expression for
 the area of the large square.
 c) What is the length of one side of the large square?
 d) Explain how this shows that $9x^2 = (3x)^2$

5 Pens cost x pence each.
 Pencils cost y pence each.
 Write down an expression for the cost in pence of:
 a) 3 pens   **b)** 8 pencils   **c)** 5 pens and 6 pencils   **d)** n pens

6 Pears cost p pence each.
Apricots cost a pence each.
Write down an expression for the cost in pence of:
   b) 2 pears   **b)** 7 apricots   **c)** 8 pears and 1 apricot

7 A small bottle of cola costs c pence.
A large bottle of cola costs three times as much as the small bottle of cola.
Write down an expression for the cost in pence of:
   a) a large bottle of cola
   b) 8 large bottles of cola
   c) 2 small bottles of cola and 5 large bottles of cola.

 EXERCISE 5.2

1 Simplify:
   a) $a + a + a$ **b)** $2b + 5b + 6b$ **c)** $3c + c + 2c + c$
   d) $4d + 2d + 5d - 3d$ **e)** $8e + e - 3e$ **f)** $12f - f - 2f - 4f$
   g) $2g + 5g - 10g$ **h)** $h - 5h$ **i)** $2i - 4i - 6i + 5i$

2 Simplify:
   a) $a + 5 + a + 3$ **b)** $2b + 7 + b + 3$ **c)** $6c + 5 - 2c - 1$
   d) $d + 6 + 2 - 3d$ **e)** $8 + 4e - 3e - 6$ **f)** $7f - 1 - 7f + 1$

3 Simplify:
   a) $a + a + b + b + a$ **b)** $2c + d + 3c + d$ **c)** $5e + 4f - 2e + 3f$
   d) $5g + 2h + 3h - g$ **e)** $3j - 2k + 5k - 2j$ **f)** $7m - 3n - 4m + 5n$
   g) $2p - 3q + 9p - 4q$ **h)** $4s - 7t - s - t$

4 Simplify:
   a) $a^2 + a^2 + a^2$ **b)** $b^2 + 6b^2 + 3b^2 + b^2$ **c)** $2c^2 + 5c^2 - c^2$
   d) $2d^3 + 2d^3 + 8d^3 - 3d^3$ **e)** $e^2 + e + 5e^2 + 4e$ **f)** $6f^2 - 4 - f^2 + 15$
   g) $3g^2 + 3g^2 - 2g^2 - 4g^2$ **h)** $h^2 - 2h^2 - 3h^2 + 8h^2 - h^2$

5 The width of this rectangle is x cm
The length is 5 cm more than the width.
   a) Write down an expression for the length of the rectangle.

The perimeter of the rectangle is found using the formula:
     Perimeter = width + length + width + length

   b) Write down an expression, in terms of x, for the perimeter of the rectangle.
      Simplify your expression.

   c) What is the perimeter of the rectangle when $x = 4$?

x cm

6 Here are three boxes of books.
The medium box contains x books.
The medium box contains 12 more
books than the small box.

Small   Medium   Large

a) Write down an expression, in terms of x,
for the number of books in the small box.

The large box contains twice as many books as the medium box.

b) Write down an expression, in terms of x, for the number of books in the large box.

c) Write down an expression, in terms of x, for the **total** number of books in all three
boxes. Simplify your expression.

d) What is the total number of books when $x = 20$?

 EXERCISE 5.3

1 Expand the following brackets:
  a) $3(a + 4)$ **b)** $6(b - 2)$ **c)** $5(2 - c)$
  d) $-9(d + 2)$ **e)** $4(3 + e)$ **f)** $-7(f - 1)$
  g) $-5(3 + g)$ **h)** $2(h - 9)$ **i)** $8(3 - i)$
  j) $-6(j - 3)$ **k)** $-4(2 + k)$ **l)** $7(m + 1)$

2 Expand the following brackets:
  a) $-2(3a + 7)$ **b)** $5(6 - 4b)$ **c)** $3(9c - 5)$
  d) $-4(8 - 5d)$ **e)** $-7(2 + 3e)$ **f)** $6(5 + 3f)$
  g) $10(-g + 4)$ **h)** $-8(6h - 1)$ **i)** $-(7 + 2i)$
  j) $-9(5j - 2)$ **k)** $2(9k + 4)$ **l)** $4(4 - m)$

3 Multiply out the brackets and simplify the results.
  a) $3(x + 7) + 4(x + 1)$ **b)** $8(x + 2) + 5(x - 2)$
  c) $9(x + 1) + 5(x + 2)$ **d)** $6(5x - 2) + 9(2x + 3)$
  e) $8(3x + 2) + 2(4x + 3)$ **f)** $5(3x + 2) + 4(3x - 2)$
  g) $6(x + 6) + 7(3x + 7)$ **h)** $7(x - 1) + 4(2x - 1)$
  i) $4(3x + 2) + 5(2x + 3)$ **j)** $9(8x - 2) + 3(3x + 4)$

4 Multiply out the brackets and simplify the results.
Take special care when there is a negative number in front of the second bracket.
  a) $5(6x - 1) + 8(2x - 5)$ **b)** $2(6x + 5) - (8x + 9)$
  c) $7(x + 9) + 3(x + 2)$ **d)** $4(4x + 3) - 2(x - 8)$
  e) $3(5x + 7) - 2(3x + 5)$ **f)** $8(x + 2) + 5(x - 7)$
  g) $9(3x - 4) - 9(2x - 7)$ **h)** $6(x - 1) - 4(5x + 2)$
  i) $10(x + 1) + 7(8x - 1)$ **j)** $11x - 6(3x - 7) + 5x$

 EXERCISE 5.4

1 Expand:
  a) $a(a + 5)$ **b)** $b(b - 2)$ **c)** $c(c + 9)$
  d) $d(7 + d)$ **e)** $e(8 - e)$ **f)** $f(3f - 4)$
  g) $g(3 - 2g)$ **h)** $h(5h + 3)$ **i)** $i(7 - 6i)$

2 Expand:
  a) $7a(a-2)$ **b)** $4b(3b+5)$ **c)** $6c(3-c)$
  d) $5d(7+4d)$ **e)** $9e(e+3)$ **f)** $2f(8-f)$
  g) $8g(7g-3)$ **h)** $3h(10h+1)$ **i)** $4i(11-6i)$

3 Expand and simplify these brackets.
   You must show all the steps in your working.
  a) $(x+5)(x+2)$ **b)** $(x+9)(x+3)$ **c)** $(x-6)(x+4)$
  d) $(x+8)(x-1)$ **e)** $(x-7)(x-2)$ **f)** $(x+6)(x+5)$
  g) $(x-3)(x+7)$ **h)** $(x-2)(x-1)$ **i)** $(x+5)(x-7)$
  j) $(x+9)(x+6)$ **k)** $(x-4)(x-4)$ **l)** $(x-3)(x+2)$

4 A large rectangle is divided into four smaller
   rectangles labelled **A**, **B**, **C** and **D**.
   The length of one side of the large rectangle
   is $(c+7)$ cm
   The length of the other side of the large
   rectangle is $(c+5)$ cm

	c	7
c	**A**	**B**
5	**C**	**D**

  a) One of the shapes is a square.
      Write down an expression for the area of this square.
  b) Write down an expression in terms of c for the area of:
      (i) rectangle **B**   **(ii)** rectangle **C**   **(iii)** rectangle **D**
  c) Write down an expression for the total area of the large rectangle.
      Simplify your expression.

5 Expand:
  a) $(a+5)^2$ **b)** $(b-6)^2$ **c)** $(c-4)^2$ **d)** $(d+4)^2$

EXERCISE 5.5

1 Factorise these expressions:
  a) $5a-10$ **b)** $12b+3$ **c)** $21c-7$
  d) $9d+63$ **e)** $5-40e$ **f)** $6+3f$

2 Factorise these expressions:
  a) $6+9a$ **b)** $10b-20$ **c)** $8c+6$
  d) $20-4d$ **e)** $12e-18$ **f)** $16+24f$

3 Factorise these expressions:
  a) $7a+ab$ **b)** $xy-x$ **c)** $5c+cd$
  d) $3xy+2y$ **e)** $4de+6e$ **f)** $10e-15de$

4 Factorise these expressions:
  a) a^2+9a **b)** b^2-3b **c)** $7c-c^2$
  d) $8d^2-d$ **e)** e^2+12e **f)** $12f-f^2$
  g) $6x^2+3xy$ **h)** $21y^2+14y$ **i)** $4hk-2h^2$

U2 CHAPTER 6

Number sequences

All the Exercises in this Chapter are Stage 1 only.

 EXERCISE 6.1

1 Here are the first three patterns in a sequence of patterns made from sticks:

Pattern 1   Pattern 2   Pattern 3

a) Draw Pattern 4
b) Copy and complete the table.

Pattern number	1	2	3	4	5
Number of sticks	3	5	7		

c) Explain how you would work out the number of sticks in Pattern 6
d) Work out how many sticks there are in Pattern 15

2 The diagram shows how tables are arranged in a hall.
x shows where a chair is placed.

Table 1   Table 2   Table 3

The rest of the tables in the hall follow the same pattern.
a) Draw Table 4
b) Copy and complete the table.

Table number	1	2	3	4	5
Number of chairs	6	10	14		

c) Explain how you would work out the number of chairs at Table 6
d) Work out how many chairs at Table 12

3 Here are the first three patterns in a sequence of patterns made from sticks.

P 1   P 2   P 3

a) Draw P4
b) Copy and complete the table.

P	1	2	3	4	5
Number of sticks	6	11	16		

c) Work out how many sticks there are in P8
d) Can a pattern be made from exactly 162 sticks? Explain your answer.

4 Here is a pattern made from squares. Each square has four edges.

Pattern 1   Pattern 2   Pattern 3

  a) Draw Pattern 4
  b) Copy and complete the table.

Pattern number	1	2	3	4	5
Number of edges	20	36	52		
Number of squares	5	9	13		

  c) Explain how you would work out the number of edges and the number of squares in Pattern 6
  d) Work out how many **(i)** edges, **(ii)** squares there are in Pattern 10

5 A pattern is made from circles and squares.

Pattern 1   Pattern 2   Pattern 3

  a) Draw Pattern 4
  b) Copy and complete the table.

Pattern number	1	2	3	4	5	10	20
Number of squares	1	2	3				
Number of circles	4	8	12				
Total squares + circles	5	10	15				

  c) Which Pattern has 60 circles?
  d) Which Pattern has a total of 200 squares + circles?

EXERCISE 6.2 **1**

1 Write down the first five terms of the number sequences generated by each of these rules.
  a) The first term is 6
    To find the next term add 7 to the previous term.
  b) The first term is 3
    To find the next term multiply the previous term by 4
  c) The first term is 28
    To find the next term subtract 4 from the previous term.

d) The first term is 486
   To find the next term divide the previous term by 3
e) The first term is 7
   To find the next term subtract 1 from the previous term.
f) The first term is 3
   To find the next term double the previous term.
g) The first term is 7
   To find the next term, double the previous term and add 6

2 For each sequence: **(i)** write down the next two terms
   (ii) explain the rule in words.
   a) $4, 6, 8, 10, 12 \ldots$ **b)** $5, 10, 15, 20, 25 \ldots$ **c)** $24, 21, 18, 15, 12 \ldots$
   d) $70, 63, 56, 49, 42 \ldots$ **e)** $6, 10, 14, 18 \ldots$ **f)** $15, 9, 3, -3, -9 \ldots$

3 Find the missing terms in these number sequences.
   a) $3, 7, ?, 15, ?, ?$ **b)** $?, 5, 8, 11, ?, ?$
   c) $15, ?, ?, 21, 23, 25, ?$ **d)** $39, ?, ?, 30, 27, 24, ?$
   e) $?, ?, ?, 18, 23, 28, 33$ **f)** $9, ?, 5, ?, ?, -1, -3, -5$

4 (i) Write down the next term in the following sequences.
   (ii) Describe how you found the next term.
   a) $1, 8, 27, 64, \ldots$ **b)** $1, 3, 9, 27, 81, \ldots$
   c) $2, 2, 4, 6, 10, 16, \ldots$ **d)** $49, 36, 25, 16, 9, \ldots$
   e) $3, 5, 8, 12, 17, 23 \ldots$ **f)** $64, 32, 16, 8 \ldots$

5 Look at this number sequence: $3, 7, 11, 15, 19, \ldots$
   a) Write down the next three terms in the sequence.
   b) Explain how you found your answer.

   The 50th term of the sequence is 199
   c) Write down the 51st term.
   d) Will 500 be a term in this sequence?
      Explain your answer.

6 Andy has been doing an investigational GCSE coursework task.
   He gets this sequence of numbers:

   $$12, 17, 22, 27, 32, \ldots$$

   a) Write down the next three terms in Andy's number sequence.
   b) Write a rule for Andy's number sequence.

7 Emily has been working with odd numbers.
   Emily is not quite right.
   Rewrite Emily's statement
   so that it is correct.

The rule for odd numbers is: 'add 2 to the previous term'

Emily

8 Look at this number sequence: 2, 5, 8, 11, 14, …
  a) Write down the next three terms in the sequence.
  b) Explain how you found your answer.

  The 50th term of the sequence is 149
  c) Write down the 51st term.
  d) Will 99 be a term in this sequence? Explain your answer.

9 Look at this number sequence: 7, 13, 19, 25, 31, …
  a) Write down the next three terms in the sequence.
  b) Explain how you found your answer.

  The 100th term of the sequence is 601
  c) Write down the 101st term.
  d) Will 100 be a term in this sequence? Explain your answer.

EXERCISE 6.3

1 Write down the first five terms of the following sequences:
  a) nth term $= 5n$ 　　**b)** nth term $= 6n$ 　　**c)** nth term $= n - 1$
  d) nth term $= n + 2$ 　　**e)** nth term $= n + 4$ 　　**f)** nth term $= n - 5$
  g) nth term $= 2n + 1$ 　　**h)** nth term $= 3n - 1$

2 The nth term of a number sequence is given by the formula $4n - 3$
  a) Write down the first five terms of the number sequence.
  b) Work out the 20th term.

3 The nth term of a number sequence is given by the formula $\frac{1}{2}(10n + 3)$
  a) Write down the first five terms of the number sequence.
  b) Work out the 10th term.

4 Write down the first five terms of the following sequences:
  a) nth term $= n^3 - 1$
  b) nth term $= n^2 + 1$
  c) nth term $= 2n^2$
  d) nth term $= n^3 + n^2$

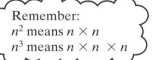
Remember:
n^2 means $n \times n$
n^3 means $n \times n \times n$

5 The nth term of a number sequence is given by the formula $\dfrac{n^2 + 2}{2}$
  a) Write down the first five terms of the number sequence.
  b) Work out the 30th term.

EXERCISE 6.4

1 Find an expression for the nth term of the following sequences:
  a) 3, 6, 9, 12, 15, … 　　　　　**b)** 5, 10, 15, 20, 25, …
  c) 8, 16, 24, 32, 40, … 　　　　**d)** 11, 22, 33, 44, 55, …
  e) 100, 200, 300, 400, 500, … 　**f)** 20, 40, 60, 80, 100, …

2 Find an expression for the nth term of the following sequences:
  a) 5, 8, 11, 14, 17, … 　　　　　**b)** 4, 9, 14, 19, 24, …
  c) 3, 7, 11, 15, 19, … 　　　　　**d)** 5, 7, 9, 11, 13, …
  e) 13, 23, 33, 43, 53, … 　　　　**f)** 5, 12, 19, 26, 33, …

3 Find an expression for the nth term of the following sequences:
  a) $9, 7, 5, 3, 1, \ldots$ **b)** $20, 16, 12, 8, 4, \ldots$
  c) $90, 80, 70, 60, 50, \ldots$ **d)** $23, 20, 17, 14, 11, \ldots$

4 The first five terms in an arithmetic sequence are:

   $8, 14, 20, 26, 32, \ldots$

  a) Find the value of the tenth term. **b)** Write a formula for the nth term.

5 The first four terms in an arithmetic sequence are:

   $43, 38, 33, 28, 23, \ldots$

  a) Find the value of the first negative term.
  b) Write a formula for the nth term.

6 Robert has been making patterns with sticks.
  Here are his first three patterns.

  a) Draw Pattern 4
  b) Work out the number of
  sticks in Pattern 5

  Pattern 1   Pattern 2   Pattern 3

  c) Give a formula for the number of sticks, s, in Pattern n
  d) Explain how your formula relates to the way the sticks fit together.

7 The seventh term of an arithmetic sequence is 34 and the eighth term is 40
  a) Write down the value of the common difference for this sequence.
  b) Work out the value of the first term.
  c) Find an expression for the nth term of the sequence.
    Check that your expression works when $n = 5$ and $n = 6$

EXERCISE 6.5 ❶

Do not use your calculator for Questions 1–3.

1 Look at this pattern of trapeziums made from sticks.

   Pattern 1   Pattern 2   Pattern 3

  a) Draw the next pattern.
  b) Copy and complete the table.
  c) How many sticks would
  there be in Pattern 7?

Pattern number	1	2	3	4	5
Number of sticks	5	9	13		

  d) Find a formula for the number of
  sticks, S, in Pattern n

2 (i) Write down the next two terms in each of these number sequences.
  (ii) Find the 10th term.
  (iii) Give a formula for the nth term in each case.
  a) $0, 3, 8, 15, 24, \ldots$ **b)** $3, 6, 11, 18, 27, \ldots$
  c) $8, 11, 16, 23, 32, \ldots$ **d)** $11, 14, 19, 26, 35, \ldots$
  e) $201, 204, 209, 216, 225, \ldots$ **f)** $-4, -1, 4, 11, 20, \ldots$

3 Here are the first three patterns in a sequence of patterns made from hexagons.

Pattern 1   Pattern 2   Pattern 3

a) Draw Pattern 4

Pattern number	1	2	3	4	5
Number of black hexagons	2	3	4		
Number of white hexagons	2	4	6		
Total number of hexagons	4	7	10		

b) Copy and complete the table.
c) Work out the **total** number of hexagons in Pattern 10
d) Find a formula for the **total** number of hexagons, H, in Pattern n

4 To work out a rule for the nth term in this pattern, we can put two trapeziums together to make rectangles like this:

                  1   2   3   4

No. of dots in rectangle: $1 \times 2 = 2$ $2 \times 4 = 8$ $3 \times 6 = ?$ $? \times ? = ?$

No. of dots in trapezium: $\dfrac{1 \times 2}{2} = 1$ $\dfrac{2 \times 4}{2} = 4$ $\dfrac{3 \times 6}{2} = ?$ $\dfrac{? \times ?}{2} = ?$

a) How many dots are there in rectangle:
   (i) 3   **(ii)** 4   **(iii)** 5?
b) How many dots are there in trapezium:
   (i) 3   **(ii)** 4   **(iii)** 5?
c) Carrying on the pattern:
   (i) the 10th rectangle would have $10 \times (10 + 10) = ?$ dots

   (ii) the 10th trapezium would have $\dfrac{10 \times (? + ?)}{2} = ?$ dots

   (iii) the nth rectangle would have $? \times (? + ?)$ dots

   (iv) the nth trapezium would have $\dfrac{? \times (? + ?)}{?}$ dots.

Fill in the missing values.

U2 CHAPTER 7

Coordinates and graphs

Exercises 7.1, 7.2 and 7.3 are Stage 1. All Exercises are Stage 2.

 EXERCISE 7.1

1 Write down the coordinates of the points A to H.

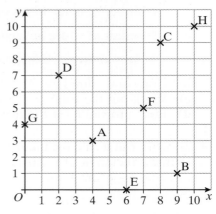

2 Write down the coordinates of the points A to H.

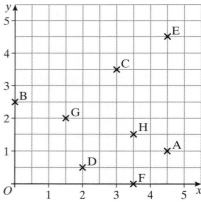

3 a) Write down the coordinates of:
   (i) A   **(ii)** B.

   b) Write down the coordinates of the midpoint of the line segment AB.

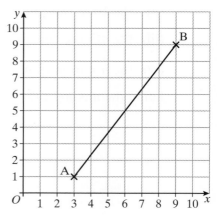

4 Draw a pair of axes on a grid and label both axes from 0 to 10
  a) Plot the points A(7, 1) and B(1, 9)
  Join the points with a straight line.
  b) Mark the midpoint, M, of the line segment AB.
  c) Write down the coordinates of M.

5 Draw a pair of axes on a grid and label both axes from 0 to 7
  a) Plot the points A(2, 1), B(6, 1), C(6, 5), and D(2, 5)
  b) Join the points in order, to form a closed shape.
  c) What is the name of the shape?

  Mark the centre, M, of your shape.
  d) Write down the coordinates of M.

6 Draw a pair of axes on a grid and label both axes from 0 to 6
  a) Plot the points A(1, 2), B(6, 2) and C(6, 5). Join A to B and B to C.

  A fourth point, D, is needed to form a rectangle.
  b) Write down the coordinates of D.

7 The point A has coordinates (9, 4)
  The point B has coordinates (3, 6)
  M is the midpoint of the line segment AB.
  Find the coordinates of M.

8 The point A has coordinates (14, 3)
  The point B has coordinates (4, 11)
  M is the midpoint of the line segment AB.
  Find the coordinates of M.

EXERCISE 7.2

1 Using the diagram, write down the
   coordinates of A, B, C, D and E.

2 a) Which point is at $(-4, -2)$?
  b) What are the coordinates of L?
  c) Which point is midway between $(2, -6)$ and $(8, 0)$?
  d) What are the coordinates of H?
  e) Which point has the **largest** y coordinate?
  f) Which point has the **smallest** x coordinate?
  g) Which point has the **same** x coordinate and y coordinate?

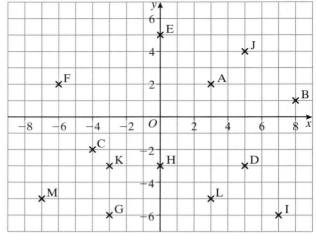

3 Draw a pair of axes on a grid and label both axes from -4 to 4
  a) Plot the points $A(-1, 4)$ and $B(3, -2)$
  b) Join the points with a straight line.
    Mark the midpoint, M, of the line segment AB.
  c) Write down the coordinates of M.

4 Draw a pair of axes on a grid and label both axes from -4 to 5
  a) Plot the points $A(5, 1), B(5, -3), C(-1, -3)$, and $D(-1, 1)$
  b) Join the points in order, to form a closed shape.
  c) What is the name of the shape?
  d) Mark the centre, M, of your shape.
    Write down the coordinates of M.

5 Draw a pair of axes on a grid and label both axes from -6 to 6
  a) Plot the points $A(3, 2), B(-1, 2)$ and $C(-3, -2)$. Join A to B and B to C.
  b) A fourth point, D, is needed to form a parallelogram.
    Write down the coordinates of D.
  c) Mark the centre, M, of your shape.
    Write down the coordinates of M.

6 The point A has coordinates $(8, -2)$. The point B has coordinates $(-4, -6)$
  M is the midpoint of the line segment AB. Find the coordinates of M.

7 The point A has coordinates $(-8, 0)$. The point B has coordinates $(4, -6)$
  M is the midpoint of the line segment AB. Find the coordinates of M.

8 Follow these instructions carefully.
  Draw a coordinate grid and label both axes from -10 to 10 on the x axis and -4 to 4 on the y axis. Now draw line segments as follows:

From $(-8, 3)$ to $(-8, -3)$	From $(0, 3)$ to $(4, 3)$
From $(-8, 0)$ to $(-5, 3)$	From $(6, 3)$ to $(6, -3)$
From $(-8, 0)$ to $(-5, -3)$	From $(6, 3)$ to $(9, 3)$
From $(-2, 3)$ to $(-2, -3)$	From $(6, 0)$ to $(8, 0)$
From $(2, 3)$ to $(2, -3)$	From $(6, -3)$ to $(9, -3)$

  You should find that you have named a 4-sided shape. Draw a sketch of this shape.

EXERCISE 7.3 pt ① ②

Write down the coordinates of the **vertices** (corners) on each of these cuboids.

1

2

3

4

5

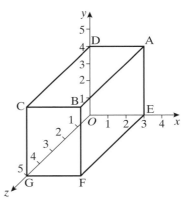

EXERCISE 7.4 pt ②

1 Write down the equation of each of the lines labelled A to E.

2 Draw a pair of axes on a grid and label both axes from −6 to 6
Draw these lines and label them with their letter:

  a) $x = 3$ **b)** $y = 2$ **c)** $x = -4$

  d) $y = -5$ **e)** $y = x$ **f)** $x = -y$

3 Write down an equation for the **a)** x axis and **b)** y axis.

For Questions **4** to **10**, complete the table of values for the given equation and draw the graph. A rough set of axes next to each question shows you how to draw your axes.

4 $y = x + 1$

x	0	1	2	3	4
y	1		3		5

5 $y = 2x + 1$

x	0	1	2	3	4
y	1	3			9

6 $y = 4x$

x	0	1	2	3	4
y	0	4		12	

7 $y = 3x - 2$

x	0	1	2	3	4
y	-2	1			10

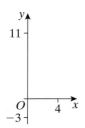

8 $y = 2x - 1$

x	-2	-1	0	1	2
y		-3			3

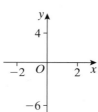

9 $y = 4 - x$

x	-2	-1	0	1	2
y		5		3	

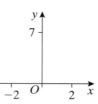

10 $x + y = 5$

x	0	1	2	3	4	5
y			3	2		

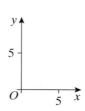

11 a) Draw a pair of axes so that:
the x values start at 0 and end at 5
the y values start at 0 and end at 10
b) Draw the graph of $y = x + 4$
c) Use your graph to find:
  (i) the value of y when $x = 2.3$
  (ii) the value of x when $y = 7.8$

12 a) Draw a pair of axes so that:
the x values start at 0 and end at 5
the y values start at 0 and end at 18
b) Draw the graph of $y = 3x + 1$
c) Use your graph to find:
  (i) the value of y when $x = 2.7$
  (ii) the value of x when $y = 12.5$

13 a) Draw a pair of axes so that:
the x values start at -4 and finish at 4
the y values start at -4 and finish at 8
b) Draw the graph of $x + y = 2$
c) Use your graph to find:
  (i) the value of y when $x = 3.5$
  (ii) the value of x when $y = 2.8$

14 Draw the following graphs:
a) $y = x + 6$ for $0 \leqslant x \leqslant 4$
b) $y = 2x$ for $0 \leqslant x \leqslant 4$
c) $y = 4x - 1$ for $0 \leqslant x \leqslant 4$

EXERCISE 7.5

1 This conversion graph
converts between kilometres
and miles.

a) Harry travels 6 kilometres.
What is this distance
in miles?

b) Kate travels 2 miles.
What is this distance in
kilometres?

c) The distance between the
church and the school is
4.3 kilometres.
What is this distance
in miles?

d) Rick walks 4.3 miles.
How far does he walk in kilometres?

e) Paul jogs 5 kilometres.
How far is this in miles?

f) Mary wants to convert 0.8 miles to kilometres.
What is 0.8 miles in kilometres?

2 This conversion graph converts the temperature in Celsius to the temperature in Fahrenheit.

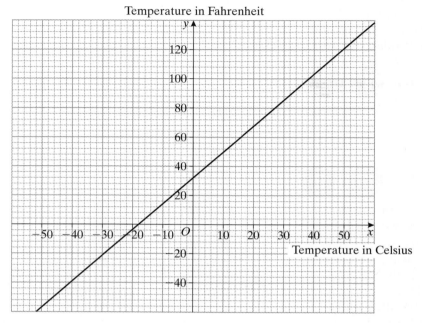

Temperature in Fahrenheit

Temperature in Celsius

a) Use the graph to convert 0 °C to °F

b) Diana went to Spain. The temperature when she arrived was 28 °C
What is 28 °C in degrees Fahrenheit?

3 a) Use the fact that 10 litres ≈ 17.5 pints to produce a conversion graph between litres and pints.

b) Use your graph to convert:
    (i) 10 pints   **(ii)** 6 pints to litres.

c) Use your graph to convert:
    (i) 7 litres   **(ii)** 2 litres to pints.

U2 CHAPTER 8

Measurements

Exercises 8.1, 8.2 and 8.3 are Stage 1. All Exercises are Stage 2.

EXERCISE 8.1

Do not use your calculator for Questions 1–4.

1 Change these times to the 24 hour clock times.

a)

am

b)

pm

c)

pm

d)

am

e)

am

f)

pm

2 These digital clocks are showing 24 hour clock times.

| 15:18 | 07:28 | 20:20 | 16:51 | 03:49 | 10:09 |

Change them to 12 hour clock times.
Don't forget to write 'am' or 'pm'.

3 The time is 9.52 am.
George had to wait another 4 hours and 23 minutes for his favourite
TV programme.
What time is George's TV programme?

4 Peter finishes school at 15 40
It is now 13 52
How much longer must Peter wait before school finishes?

You can use your calculator for Questions 5–9.

5 Change these hours to minutes:
  a) 3 hours
  b) 1.5 hours
  c) $\frac{1}{4}$ of an hour
  d) 0.75 hours
  e) 2.3 hours
  f) 5.8 hours

6 Change these minutes to hours:
  a) 240 minutes
  b) 600 minutes
  c) 130 minutes
  d) 90 minutes
  e) 20 minutes
  f) 135 minutes

7 Look at this digital clock. `19:48`

What should the display show in:
a) $\frac{1}{4}$ of an hour's time?   b) $2\frac{1}{2}$ hours' time?   c) $1\frac{3}{4}$ hours' time?

8 Here is part of a bus timetable.

Esther catches the 10 31 bus from Sparrow Lane.
a) At what time should the bus arrive at Robin Crescent?

Chris arrives at the High Street at 9.59 am
b) (i) How long should Chris expect to wait for a bus to take him to Hawk Road?
(ii) How long should Chris expect the bus journey to take?

High Street	09 23	09 53	10 26	10 50
Sparrow Lane	09 28	09 58	10 31	–
Raven Avenue	09 37	–	–	–
Seagull End	09 45	–	10 46	11 02
Hawk Road	09 52	–	–	11 09
Robin Crescent	10 02	10 28	11 00	11 19

9 Here is part of a train timetable.

Carol plans to catch the 20 48 from Highville to go to Lowden.
a) How long should Carol expect the journey to take?

Carol doesn't arrive at Highville station until 20 56
b) What time should Carol expect to arrive in Lowden?

Highville	19 52	20 14	20 48	21 06
Smalltown	20 12	–	21 08	21 26
Largeford	20 17	20 35	–	–
Littlewood	20 32	20 40	–	21 42
Bighampton	20 48	–	–	21 58
Lowden	21 02	21 08	21 36	22 13

EXERCISE 8.2

1 Write down a sensible metric unit that could be used to measure:
a) the length of a shoe   b) the distance between London and Brighton
c) the length of a pencil   d) the weight of a pen
e) the height of a block of flats   f) the capacity of a teaspoon
g) the weight of your friend   h) the length of an ant
i) the amount of wine in a large barrel
j) the weight of an elephant   k) the length of a classroom
l) the capacity of a cup

2 Convert the following measurements to metres:
a) 3546 mm   b) 423 cm   c) 6 km   d) 85 cm   e) 0.7 km
f) 135 cm   g) 7.1 km   h) 23 km   i) 4 cm

3 Change the following measurements to centimetres:
a) 7 m   b) 23 mm   c) 7 mm   d) 8.3 m   e) 92 mm
f) 769 mm   g) 16.3 mm   h) 6.25 m i) 0.578 m

4 Change the following measurements:
  a) 2.9 tonnes to kilograms
  c) 0.26 kilograms to grams
  e) 8.05 kilograms to grams

  b) 20 kilograms to tonnes
  d) 7.2 kilograms to grams
  f) 800 grams to kilograms

5 Change the following measurements:
  a) 7 litres to millilitres
  c) 520 millilitres to centilitres
  e) 0.9 litres to millilitres

  b) 8904 millilitres to litres
  d) 8.12 litres to centilitres
  f) 64 centilitres to litres

6 Convert the following measurements:
  a) 200 metres to kilometres
  c) 34 centimetres to millimetres
  e) 76 centimetres to millimetres

  b) 9000 metres to kilometres
  d) 4701 metres to kilometres
  f) 5 metres to millimetres

7 Write down sensible estimates using appropriate metric units for:
  a) the length and width of your bedroom
  c) the height of a popstar
  e) the capacity of a bottle of shampoo
  g) the length of your toothbrush

  b) the height of bedroom door
  d) the weight of a popstar
  f) the weight of an egg
  h) the weight of 10 apples

EXERCISE 8.3 **1** **2**

Do not use your calculator for Questions 1–3.

1 Write down a sensible imperial unit that could be used to measure:
  a) the height of a two storey house
  b) the length of a garden
  c) the weight of a baby sparrow
  d) the distance between Glasgow and London
  e) the length of a pen
  f) the volume of milk in a large carton
  g) the weight of a sack of potatoes

2 Change:
  a) 150 miles to kilometres
  c) 320 kilometres to miles
  e) 24 kilometres to miles

  b) 500 miles to kilometres
  d) 30 miles to kilometres
  f) 40 kilometres to miles

3 Change:
  a) 20 centimetres to inches
  c) 18 litres to gallons
  e) 40 gallons to litres

  b) 4 litres to pints
  d) 120 centimetres to feet
  f) 36 feet to metres

You can use your calculator for Questions 4–7.

4 Change:
  a) 55 miles to kilometres
  c) 42 pints to litres
  e) 80 miles to kilometres

  b) 18 gallons to litres
  d) 24 inches to centimetres
  f) 35 kilograms to pounds

5 Jason is 6 feet 4 inches tall.
   a) Change:
       (i) 6 feet to metres   **(ii)** 4 inches to centimetres
   b) What is Jason's height in metres?

   Jason weighs 160 lb
   c) What is Jason's weight in kilograms?
       Give your answer correct to 2 significant figures.

6 Steve buys 10 gallons of beer for a party.
   Approximately how many litres of beer does Steve buy?

7 Johnny drives 370 miles.
   What is 370 miles in kilometres?

EXERCISE 8.4

Do not use your calculator for Questions 1–7.

1 Lisa cycles 40 miles in 5 hours.
   What is her average speed?

2 A car travels 50 miles in one hour 15 minutes.
   What is the average speed of the car in miles per hour?

3 David cycles for 2 hours at an average speed of 10 km/h
   How far does David cycle?

4 Martin drives 200 km at an average speed of 40 km/h
   How long does the journey take?

5 A car travels 3 hours at an average speed of 120 km/h
   How far does the car travel?

6 A car travels for 8 hours at an average speed of 50 mph
   How far does the car travel?

7 Michelle jogs for 30 minutes at an average speed of 7 km/h
   How far does Michelle jog?

You can use your calculator for Questions 8–11.

8 Ian jogs for 40 minutes at an average speed of 80 metres per minute.
   How far does Ian run?

9 Debbie drives 120 km at an average speed of 100 km/h
   How long in minutes does the journey take?

10 Robert runs 100 metres in 20 seconds.
   a) What is his average speed in metres per second?
   b) What is Robert's average speed in kilometres per hour?

11 An intercity train travels at 160 km/h
- **a)** How far does it travel in:
  - **(i)** 30 minutes   **(ii)** 45 minutes   **(iii)** 1 hour 15 minutes?
- **b)** How long in minutes does it take to travel:
  - **(i)** 80 km   **(ii)** 8 km   **(iii)** 200 km?
- **c)** What is the speed of the train in metres per second?
  Give your answer correct to 1 decimal place.

EXERCISE 8.5 **2**

1 The density of water is 1000 kg/m^3
- **a)** Find the mass of:
  - **(i)** 30 m^3 of water **(ii)** 0.4 m^3 of water **(iii)** 0.6 m^3 of water **(iv)** 8 m^3 of water
- **b)** What is the volume of:
  - **(i)** 500 kg of water **(ii)** 750 kg of water **(iii)** 2500 kg of water **(iv)** 4000 kg of water?

You can use your calculator for Questions 2 and 3.

2 An aluminium hubcap has a volume of 2620 cm^3
   The mass of the hubcap is 720 g
   Give all your answers to 2 significant figures.
- **a)** Work out the density of aluminium in g/cm^3
- **b)** What is the mass in grams of 1 cm^3 of aluminium?
- **c)** What is the mass in grams of 1 m^3 of aluminium?
- **d)** What is the mass in kilograms of 1 m^3 of aluminium?
- **e)** What is the density of aluminium in kg/m^3?

3 The density of silver is 10.49 g/cm^3
   Give all your answers to 3 significant figures.
- **a)** Find the volume of silver used to make a silver ring of mass 35 g
- **b)** Find the volume of silver used to make a silver spoon of mass 200 g

   A silver coin has a volume of 3 cm^3
- **c)** What is the mass of the coin?

EXERCISE 8.6 **2**

1 These numbers have all been rounded to the nearest whole number.
   Write down their   **(i)** lower bound   **(ii)** upper bound
- **a)** 685   **b)** 3   **c)** 37   **d)** 70   **e)** 120

2 Write down the   **(i)** lower bound   **(ii)** upper bound of these measurements:
- **a)** A line that is 6 cm long to the nearest centimetre.
- **b)** A house that is 12 m long to the nearest metre.
- **c)** An orange weighing 132 g to the nearest gram.
- **d)** A woman who is 135 cm tall to the nearest centimetre.
- **e)** The distance between two towns that is 156 km to the nearest kilometre.
- **f)** A child weighing 46 kg to the nearest kilogram.

U2 CHAPTER 9

Angles

Exercises 9.1 and 9.2 are Stage 1. All Exercises are Stage 2.

 EXERCISE 9.1

1 Write down an estimate for each of the angles **a)** to **d)**

a)

b)

c)

d)

2 Measure each angle to the nearest degree.

3 For each of the following questions
(i) Work out the angles marked with letters. (ii) Give a reason for your answer.

a)

b)

c)

d)

e)

f)

g)

h)

i)

j)

k)

l)

m)

n)

o)

p)

4 Write down what type of angle (e.g. acute, obtuse, reflex) each of the following angles in question **3** is: *c, d, e, f, m, n, s, u*

EXERCISE 9.2 ❶ ❷

Find the size of each of the angles represented by the letters in each question.

1

2

3

4

5

6

7

8

9

10

11

12

13

14

15

EXERCISE 9.3

1 Measure the bearings of each of the following six towns from Gingbridge.

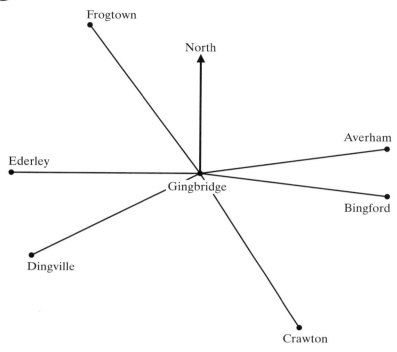

2 Write down the bearing on which a plane flies when it is flying:
   a) due South   **b)** due East   **c)** North-east   **d)** South-west.

3 Huntville is 9 km away from Ivaton on a bearing of 065°
   Make a scale drawing of the two towns. Use a scale of 1 cm to 1 km.

4 A ship is 10.8 km away from a lighthouse on a bearing of 250°
   a) Make a scale drawing of the ship and the lighthouse. Use a scale of 1 cm to 1 km

   A ferry is 15 km away from the ship on a bearing of 127°
   b) Add the position of the ferry to your scale drawing.
   c) Measure the bearing of the ferry from the lighthouse.

5 Look at this sketch. It is not drawn to scale.
   a) Write down the bearing of B from A.
   b) Work out the bearing of A from B.

6 Look at this sketch. It is not drawn to scale.
a) Work out the bearing of R from P.
b) Work out the bearing of P from R.

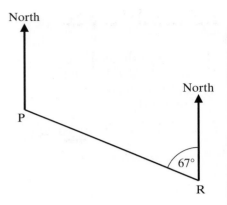

7 Abbeyton is north-west of Bonville.
a) What is the bearing of Abbeyton from Bonville?
b) What is the bearing of Bonville from Abbeyton?

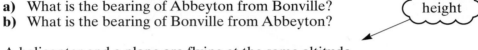

8 A helicopter and a plane are flying at the same altitude.
The bearing of the helicopter from the plane is 195°
What is the bearing of the plane from the helicopter?

9 Cogtown is on a bearing of 320° from Damston.
What is the bearing of Damston from Cogtown?

10 This sketch shows the position of three boats.
It is not a scale drawing.

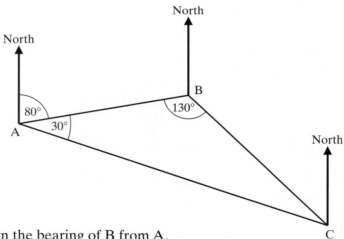

a) Write down the bearing of B from A.
b) Work out the bearing of:
  (i) A from B **(ii)** C from A **(iii)** B from C **(iv)** A from C **(v)** C from B.

U2 CHAPTER 10

2-D and 3-D shapes

Exercises 10.1, 10.2, 10.3 and 10.4 are Stage 1. All Exercises are Stage 2.

 EXERCISE 10.1

1 Name the types of triangles and quadrilaterals labelled A to M in the diagram.

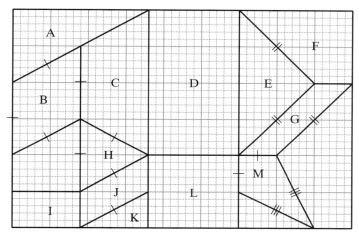

2 Two different types of quadrilaterals have all four sides the same length.
What types of quadrilaterals are these?

3 Three different quadrilaterals always have exactly two pairs of sides the same length.
What types of quadrilaterals are these?

4 A quadrilateral has all four sides the same length.

Is Mel correct?
Explain why.

> All four angles must be the same size.

Mel

5 On separate copies of this circle, draw:
   a) a diameter
   b) an arc
   c) a chord
   d) a radius.

6 On separate copies of this circle,
draw and shade:
a) a segment
b) a sector
c) a semi-circle.

 EXERCISE 10.2 **1** **2**

1 Work out: **(i)** the perimeter, **(ii)** the area of each of these rectangles.

a)

3 cm
4 cm

b)

6 m
10 m

c)

4 mm
9 mm

d)

28 cm
4 cm

 You can use your calculator for Questions 2–10.

2 Work out: **(i)** the perimeter, **(ii)** the area of each of these squares.

a)

2 cm
2 cm

b)

3.7 m
3.7 m

c)

6.4 mm

d)

9.1 cm

10 2-D and 3-D shapes U2

3 Work out: **(i)** the perimeter, **(ii)** the area of each of these triangles.

a)

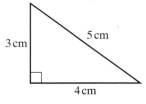

3 cm, 5 cm, 4 cm

b)

5 m, 12 m, 13 m

c)

8 mm, 5.6 mm, 8 mm, 11.4 mm

d)

10 cm, 8.66 cm, 10 cm, 10 cm

4 Work out the area of these triangles.

a)

9.7 cm, 6.5 cm

b)

4.8 m, 1.6 m

c)

8 cm, 15 cm

d)

10.1 cm, 16.2 cm

e)

4 m, 23 m

f)

8 m, 9.2 m, 7.3 m

5 Find: **a)** the area, **b)** the perimeter of this triangle.

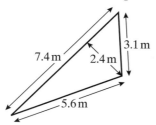

6 A rectangle has an area of 18 cm²
   Its sides are a whole number of centimetres.
   a) On squared paper, draw three different rectangles
   with an area of 18 cm²

   The perimeter of the rectangle is 22 cm
   b) What are the dimensions of the rectangle?

18 cm²

7 A square has a perimeter of 40 cm
   What is the area of the square?

The length
and width.

8 A square has an area of 81 cm²
   What is the perimeter of the square?

9 This classroom has an area of 60 m²
   a) What is the length of the classroom?
   b) What is the perimeter of the classroom?

5 m

10 A farmer puts 180 m of fencing around
   this rectangular field.
   a) What is the length of the field?
   b) What is the area of the field?

35 m

EXERCISE 10.3 **1** **2**

Do not use your calculator for Questions 1 and 2.

1 Find the area of each of these parallelograms:

a)

5 cm

12 cm

b)

6.15 m

10 m

10 2-D and 3-D shapes U2

2 Find the area of each of these trapeziums:

a)

4 cm
7 cm
12 cm

b)

13 cm
8 cm
6 cm

You can use your calculator for Question 3.

3 Find the area of each shape.

a)

7 cm
8.5 cm
10 cm

b)

14 cm
8 cm
20 cm

c)

9 m
9 m
7 m
9 m
9 m

d)

5.6 cm
4 cm
3.8 cm
4 cm
8.2 cm

EXERCISE 10.4

1 Find the shaded area of each shape.

a)

7 cm
5 cm

b)

6 cm
7 cm
9 cm

c)

3 cm
5 cm
2 cm
8 cm

d)

7 cm
3 cm
8 cm
1 cm

e)

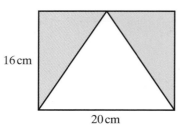

16 cm

20 cm

f)

2 cm

30 cm 18 cm 3 cm

50 cm

You can use your calculator for Questions 2 and 3.

2 Calculate: **(i)** the perimeter, **(ii)** the area of each shape. State the units in each case.

a)

7 m

4 m

2 m

9 m

b)

5 cm

8 cm

9 cm

6 cm

12 cm

c)

40 mm

18 mm 18 mm

22 mm

21 mm

10 mm

d)

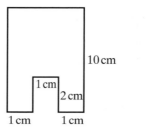

10 cm

1 cm

2 cm

1 cm 1 cm

e)

7 m

5 m

3 m

3 m

f)

18 cm

3 cm

11 cm

10 cm

3 cm

17 cm

3 Find the shaded area of each shape.

a)

6 cm

2 cm 2 cm

10 cm

b)

4.3 cm

12.1 cm

5.2 cm

13.8 cm

c)

26.7 cm
12.4 cm
←9.8 cm→
←19.2 cm→

d)

←22 cm→
25 cm
←38 cm→

 EXERCISE 10.5

Do not use your calculator for Questions 1–3.

1 Find:
  (i) the volume,
  (ii) the surface area of these shapes.

a)   **b)**   **c)**

represents
1 cm³

2 a) Draw each of these shapes on isometric paper.
  b) Find the volume of each shape.

(i)

 Represents 1 cm³

(ii)

(iii)

3 The diagram shows a cuboid, with
  dimensions 5 cm, 8 cm and 10 cm
  Calculate its **a)** surface area, **b)** volume.
  State the units in your answers.

8 cm
5 cm
10 cm

 You can use your calculator for Questions 4–8.

4 The diagram shows a prism.
  Its cross section is a right-angled triangle with sides
  6 cm, 8 cm, 10 cm
  The prism has a length of 12 cm
  a) Calculate the area of the cross section, shaded
    in the diagram.
  b) Work out the volume of the prism.
  c) Calculate the surface area of the prism.

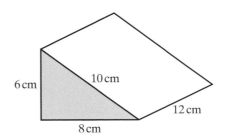

6 cm
10 cm
12 cm
8 cm

5 The cross section of a steel girder is in the shape of a letter T.
The cross section is shown in the diagram.

  a) Work out the area of the T-shaped cross section.

  The girder is 50 cm long.

  b) Work out the volume of the girder.

6 A cube measures 20 cm along each side.

  a) Work out the volume of the cube.

  b) Work out the surface area of the cube.

7 A cuboid measures 37 cm by 40 cm by 5 cm

  a) Work out the volume of the cuboid.

  b) Work out the surface area of the cuboid.

8 The diagram shows a water tank.
It is in the shape of a cuboid.
It has no lid.

  a) Work out the volume of the tank,
  correct to 3 significant figures.

  b) Work out the total surface area of the
  inside of the tank.

UNIT 3

U3 CHAPTER 1

Number review

EXERCISE 1.1

Work out the answers to these problems in your head.

1 38 + 27 + 594 + 12
2 234 + 356 + 41
3 55 + 739 + 184

4 743 + 136 + 87
5 32 + 33 + 34 + 35 + 36
6 26 + 53 + 17 + 49

7 38 + 49 + 795
8 437 − 99
9 138 + 381

10 573 − 399

Use any written method to work out the answers to these problems. Show your working clearly.

11 825 + 67
12 170 + 376
13 826 − 394

14 890 − 368
15 2647 + 3691
16 509 + 417 + 32

17 7302 − 4798
18 7007 − 3678

19 An aircraft can carry 326 passengers when all the seats are full, but today 78 of the seats are empty. How many passengers are on the aircraft today?

20 The attendances at a cinema complex were 379 (Monday), 526 (Tuesday) and 804 (Wednesday). How many people attended in total?

EXERCISE 1.2

Use short multiplication to work out the answers to these calculations.

1 235 × 5
2 482 × 7
3 384 × 3
4 168 × 9

5 514 × 6
6 690 × 7
7 723 × 8
8 888 × 4

Use any written method to work out the answers to these problems. Show your working clearly.

9 573 × 21
10 389 × 32
11 704 × 45
12 616 × 82

13 461 × 63
14 902 × 56
15 157 × 97
16 833 × 74

17 A company has 36 coaches and each coach can carry 43 passengers. How many passengers in total can all the coaches carry?

18 I have a set of 24 encyclopaedias. Each one has 288 pages.
How many pages are there in the whole set?

19 Jon buys 18 stamps at 26 pence each and 14 stamps at 47 pence each.
How much does he spend in total?

20 A cinema has 43 rows with 26 seats in each row.
Calculate the total number of seats in the cinema.

EXERCISE 1.3

Use short division to work out the answers to these calculations.
(Three of them should leave remainders.)

1 $812 \div 6$	**2** $1364 \div 4$	**3** $9279 \div 9$	**4** $6832 \div 7$
5 $6895 \div 5$	**6** $3456 \div 3$	**7** $2394 \div 8$	**8** $500 \div 6$

Use long division to work out the answers to these problems. Show your working clearly.
(Only the last two should leave remainders.)

9 $1323 \div 21$	**10** $1984 \div 16$	**11** $9750 \div 25$	**12** $7776 \div 32$
13 $6372 \div 18$	**14** $9196 \div 22$	**15** $5367 \div 31$	**16** $4055 \div 27$

17 £1164 is shared out equally between 6 people. How much does each one receive?

18 May makes 17 necklaces out of 2159 beads. Each necklace has the same number of beads.
How many beads are there on each necklace?

19 A teacher shares out 868 sheets of paper equally amongst her class of 28 students.
How many sheets of paper does each student receive?

20 Havering School has 434 students divided equally into 14 classes.
How many students are in each class?

EXERCISE 1.4

Without using a calculator, work out the answers to the following.

1 $-3 + (-4)$	**2** $9 + (-5)$	**3** $7 - (-1)$	**4** $-6 - (-2)$
5 $-7 + 3$	**6** $-9 - (6)$	**7** $-1 - -3$	**8** $-8 + -5$
9 $(2) - +3$	**10** $-5 + -5$	**11** $3 - -4$	**12** $-4 - +5$
13 $1 + -6$	**14** $-6 - -1$	**15** -2×-8	**16** $-7 \times +9$
17 5×-6	**18** $-16 \div -4$	**19** $-7 \div 7$	**20** $24 \div -8$

21 Arrange these in order of size, smallest first: $0, -9, 2, 7, -4$

22 Arrange these in order of size, smallest first: $-24, -28, 15, 25, -10$

23 What number lies midway between -18 and -32

24 What number lies one-third of the way from -5 to 25

EXERCISE 1.5

1 Work out:
  a) 3×0.7 **b)** 0.5×9 **c)** 0.2×7 **d)** 8×0.4
  e) 1.1×0.3 **f)** 0.4×0.3 **g)** 0.6×0.01 **h)** 0.07×0.05
  i) 0.09×0.02 **j)** 0.8×0.06 **k)** $0.2 \times 0.3 \times 0.7$ **l)** $0.08 \times 0.4 \times 0.1$

2 Work out:
  a) 6.27×0.3 **b)** 5.09×0.2 **c)** 2.8×3.6 **d)** 5.7×1.4
  e) 7.14×3.8 **f)** 6.71×9.2

3 Given that $28 \times 64 = 1792$, work out the values of
  a) 6.4×2.8 **b)** 0.64×28 **c)** 640×280 **d)** 0.28×6.4

4 Given that $215 \times 38 = 8170$, work out the values of
  a) 2.15×3.8 **b)** 21.5×0.38 **c)** 3.8×21.5 **d)** 380×2150

EXERCISE 1.6

1 Work out:
  a) $9 \div 0.3$ **b)** $12 \div 0.2$ **c)** $15 \div 0.5$ **d)** $7 \div 0.1$
  e) $24 \div 0.06$ **f)** $100 \div 0.05$ **g)** $35 \div 0.07$ **h)** $200 \div 0.04$

2 Work out:
  a) $0.4 \div 0.1$ **b)** $0.09 \div 0.3$ **c)** $0.25 \div 0.05$ **d)** $2.8 \div 0.7$
  e) $0.45 \div 0.09$ **f)** $5.6 \div 0.07$ **g)** $4.2 \div 0.6$ **h)** $0.53 \div 0.01$

3 Use the fact that $304 \div 19 = 16$ to work out:
  a) $30.4 \div 19$ **b)** $304 \div 1.9$ **c)** $3.04 \div 1.9$ **d)** $304 \div 0.19$

4 Use the fact that $714 \div 21 = 34$ to work out:
  a) $71.4 \div 2.1$ **b)** $7.14 \div 0.21$ **c)** $714 \div 2.1$ **d)** $71.4 \div 0.34$

EXERCISE 1.7

Don't use your calculator for Questions 1–3.

1 Write each of the following using indices:

  a) $5 \times 5 \times 5$ **b)** $7 \times 7 \times 7 \times 7 \times 7 \times 7$ **c)** $\dfrac{4 \times 4 \times 4 \times 4 \times 4}{4 \times 4 \times 4}$ **d)** $\dfrac{8 \times 8 \times 8 \times 8}{8 \times 8 \times 8}$

2 Write each of the following as a single power:

  a) $9^4 \times 9^3$ **b)** $6^8 \div 6^2$ **c)** $3^{15} \times 3^2$

  d) $\dfrac{5^9}{5^4}$ **e)** $4^7 \times 4$ **f)** $\dfrac{2^{27}}{2^{15}}$

  g) $23^8 \times 23^3$ **h)** $\dfrac{7^{25}}{7^5}$ **i)** $8^{24} \div 8^4$

3 Write each of the following as a single power:

  a) $7^3 \times 7^3 \times 7 \times 7^2$ **b)** $\dfrac{5^7 \times 5^9}{5^3}$ **c)** $\dfrac{8^5 \times 8^7}{8^{11}}$

  d) $\dfrac{4^8 \times 4^6}{4 \times 4^3}$ **e)** $\dfrac{2^{23} \times 2^2}{2^{20}}$ **f)** $\dfrac{9^{10} \times 9^5}{9^3 \times 9^2}$

You can use your calculator for Question 4.

4 Use the power button on your calculator to work out:

  a) 6^5 **b)** 2^8 **c)** 5^6 **d)** 9^4

For example, to work out
5^4 press: $\boxed{5}$ $\boxed{y^x}$ $\boxed{4}$ $\boxed{=}$

EXERCISE 1.8

Don't use your calculator for Question 1.

1 What number do these calculator screens show?
Give your answers as an ordinary number (not in standard form).

  a) $\boxed{6^{04}}$ **b)** $\boxed{9^{06}}$ **c)** $\boxed{7^{03}}$

  d) $\boxed{5.1^{05}}$ **e)** $\boxed{2.3^{-05}}$ **f)** $\boxed{1.4^{-03}}$

You can use your calculator for Questions 2 and 3.

2 Give your answers in standard form.

  a) $(2 \times 10^4) + (5 \times 10^3)$ **b)** $(5 \times 10^9) \times (7 \times 10^{-5})$
  c) $(42 \times 10^{15}) \div (6 \times 10^7)$ **d)** $(8 \times 10^5) - (8 \times 10^4)$
  e) $(3.9 \times 10^2) + (2.7 \times 10^4)$ **f)** $(3.6 \times 10^{12}) \times (2 \times 10^4)$

3 Give the answers to each of these questions as an ordinary number (not in standard form).

  a) 17^3 **b)** 230^5 **c)** $\sqrt{169} \times 30^3$ **d)** $\dfrac{50^4 + 40^5}{\sqrt{0.16}}$

U3 CHAPTER 2

Ratio and proportion

EXERCISE 2.1

1 Simplify the following ratios:
   a) 4 : 8   **b)** 6 : 9   **c)** 18 : 12   **d)** 14 : 21
   e) 25 : 10   **f)** 21 : 28   **g)** 9 : 27   **h)** 48 : 16

2 Complete these equivalent ratios:
   a) 1 : 5 = 5 : ?   **b)** 3 : 4 = 12 : ?   **c)** 2 : 7 = 6 : ?
   d) 9 : 10 = ? : 50   **e)** 5 : 8 = ? : 24   **f)** 5 : 6 = ? : 30

3 Match together the equivalent ratios:

6 : 15	4 : 8	2 : 5	5 : 2	3 : 6

20 : 8	4 : 10	1 : 2	15 : 6

EXERCISE 2.2

1 Divide £150 in the following ratios:
   a) 2 : 3   **b)** 7 : 8   **c)** 5 : 12 : 13   **d)** 3 : 5 : 7

2 Divide £120 in the following ratios:
   a) 1 : 5   **b)** 3 : 7   **c)** 3 : 4 : 5   **d)** 7 : 9 : 14

3 A 60 cm line is cut into 3 pieces in the ratio 2 : 3 : 7
   Work out the length of each piece.

4 Pete and Lian share some nuts.
   Pete takes 5 nuts for every 3 nuts that Lian takes.
   There are 48 nuts.
   How many **more** nuts does Pete take than Lian?

5 In a necklace, the ratio of silver beads to gold beads is 7 : 2
   The necklace has a total of 36 beads.
   How many gold beads are in the necklace?

6 A box of chocolates has 2 milk chocolates for every 3 plain chocolates.
   There are 40 chocolates in the box.
   Work out how many plain chocolates are in the box.

7 To make fruit squash you mix 1 part of concentrate with 5 parts of water.
   How much water is needed to make 18 litres of fruit squash?

EXERCISE 2.3

1 Jason buys 5 concert tickets for £80
How much would 7 concert tickets cost?

2 Bhavana earns £9.90 for $1\frac{1}{2}$ hours of work.
Work out how much she would earn for:
a) 30 minutes   **b)** 4 hours.

3 Here are the ingredients for making a vegetable soup for 18 people:

      6 carrots
      3 onions
      2400 ml stock
      150 g lentils
      12 g thyme

Work out how much of each ingredient is needed to make vegetable soup for
a) 9 people
b) 12 people
c) 36 people.

4 A train has 8 coaches and can seat 240 people.
Work out how many passengers a train with 10 coaches can seat.

5 In 5 months Jo earns £10 800
How much will Jo earn in a year in the same job?

6 Which of these is the best buy?

15 exercise books price £3.00	24 exercise books price £5.40

7 Sandra goes to South Africa. The exchange rate is £1 = 12 Rand.
a) How many Rand does she get for £200?

Sandra buys a wood carving for 180 Rand.
b) How much does the wood carving cost in pounds (£)?

8 Here is a recipe for orange jelly for 12 people.

      10 teaspoons gelatine
      400 g sugar
      600 ml water
      1.2 litres orange juice
      2 tablespoons lemon juice

How much of each ingredient is needed to make orange jelly for:
a) 24 people
b) 18 people?

EXERCISE 2.4 pt

1 An architect draws a floor plan of a small school. She uses a scale of $1:50$

    a) Work out the measurements, in centimetres, of the following rooms on her plan:

        (i) classroom: 5 m by 8 m

        (ii) head teacher's office: 3 m by 4 m

        (iii) dining room: 10 m by 12 m

> Remember that
> 1 m = 100 cm

    b) Work out the measurements, in metres, of the following rooms:

        (i) toilets: 6 cm by 4 cm on the plan

        (ii) hall: 8.5 cm by 9.8 cm on the plan

        (iii) kitchen: 7.1 cm by 4.7 cm on the plan.

> Remember the
> scale is $1:50$

2 A model aeroplane is made on a scale of 1 cm representing 6 m

    a) Write this scale as a ratio.

    b) Work out the length of a wing on the real aeroplane if the length of a wing on the model aeroplane is 5 cm

    c) The length of the real aeroplane is 90 m
Work out the length of the model aeroplane.

3 A map has a scale of $1:50\,000$

    a) What distance (in kilometres) is represented by a map distance of:

        (i) 4 cm   **(ii)** 20 cm

        (iii) 85 mm   **(iv)** 6.8 cm?

> Remember
> 1 km = 1000 m
>   = 100 000 cm

    b) What distance (in centimetres) on the map is represented by a real distance of:

        (i) 5 km   **(ii)** 55 km   **(iii)** 7.5 km?

U3 CHAPTER 3

Fractions

EXERCISE 3.1

1 Work out the following. Give your answer as a fraction in its simplest form:

a) $\dfrac{1}{5} + \dfrac{2}{5}$ b) $\dfrac{1}{8} + \dfrac{1}{8}$ c) $\dfrac{3}{11} + \dfrac{5}{11}$

d) $\dfrac{2}{7} + \dfrac{1}{7} + \dfrac{3}{7}$ e) $\dfrac{2}{15} + \dfrac{7}{15} + \dfrac{4}{15}$ f) $\dfrac{3}{9} + \dfrac{2}{9}$

2 Work out the following. Give your answer as a fraction in its simplest form:

a) $\dfrac{7}{11} - \dfrac{2}{11}$ b) $\dfrac{11}{12} - \dfrac{5}{12} - \dfrac{1}{12}$ c) $\dfrac{6}{7} - \dfrac{4}{7}$

d) $\dfrac{8}{15} - \dfrac{2}{15}$ e) $\dfrac{18}{25} - \dfrac{11}{25}$ f) $\dfrac{3}{5} - \dfrac{2}{5}$

3 Work out the following. Give your answer as a fraction in its simplest form:

a) $\dfrac{5}{8} + \dfrac{1}{4}$ b) $\dfrac{7}{12} - \dfrac{1}{3}$ c) $\dfrac{11}{14} - \dfrac{3}{7}$ d) $\dfrac{2}{3} + \dfrac{2}{9}$ e) $\dfrac{17}{20} - \dfrac{3}{5}$

f) $\dfrac{1}{4} + \dfrac{7}{16}$ g) $\dfrac{19}{25} - \dfrac{3}{5}$ h) $\dfrac{19}{30} - \dfrac{1}{6}$ i) $\dfrac{3}{8} + \dfrac{1}{2}$

4 Work out the following. Give your answer as a fraction in its simplest form:

a) $\dfrac{1}{5} + \dfrac{1}{2}$ b) $\dfrac{3}{8} - \dfrac{1}{3}$ c) $\dfrac{1}{4} + \dfrac{3}{7}$ d) $\dfrac{5}{6} - \dfrac{2}{3}$

e) $\dfrac{7}{9} - \dfrac{3}{4}$ f) $\dfrac{1}{6} + \dfrac{2}{5}$ g) $\dfrac{3}{5} + \dfrac{1}{4}$ h) $\dfrac{5}{7} - \dfrac{1}{3}$

i) $\dfrac{2}{5} + \dfrac{2}{3}$ j) $\dfrac{2}{3} + \dfrac{1}{2} - \dfrac{3}{4}$ k) $\dfrac{3}{5} - \dfrac{1}{3} + \dfrac{1}{4}$ l) $\dfrac{1}{3} + \dfrac{1}{4} - \dfrac{1}{2}$

5 Sarah spends $\dfrac{3}{7}$ of her monthly earnings on rent.

She spends $\dfrac{1}{7}$ of her monthly earnings on food.

a) What fraction of her monthly earnings does Sarah spend on rent and food?
b) What fraction of her monthly earnings does Sarah have left?

6 Jill spends $\dfrac{2}{5}$ of her pocket money on entertainment.

She spends $\dfrac{1}{3}$ of her pocket money on a CD.

Jill saves the rest of her pocket money.
a) What fraction of her pocket money does Jill spend?
b) What fraction of her pocket money does Jill save?

EXERCISE 3.2

1 Write the following as top-heavy fractions:

a) $1\frac{3}{5}$ b) $2\frac{1}{4}$ c) $1\frac{5}{7}$ d) $4\frac{2}{3}$ e) $5\frac{1}{6}$ f) $3\frac{1}{3}$ g) $6\frac{1}{2}$ h) $2\frac{4}{9}$

2 Write the following as mixed numbers:

a) $\frac{9}{5}$ b) $\frac{11}{3}$ c) $\frac{5}{2}$ d) $\frac{7}{4}$ e) $\frac{13}{5}$ f) $\frac{22}{7}$ g) $\frac{35}{6}$ h) $\frac{89}{10}$

3 Work out the following. Give your answer as a fraction in its simplest form:

a) $3\frac{5}{7} - 2\frac{3}{7}$ b) $1\frac{1}{4} + 2\frac{1}{4}$ c) $4\frac{2}{9} + 3\frac{5}{9}$

d) $3\frac{2}{3} - 2\frac{1}{3}$ e) $2\frac{5}{6} - 1\frac{1}{6}$ f) $1\frac{2}{5} + 2\frac{2}{5}$

4 Work out the following. Give your answer as a fraction in its simplest form:

a) $2\frac{1}{4} + 1\frac{1}{3}$ b) $1\frac{5}{6} - 1\frac{2}{3}$ c) $3\frac{1}{2} + 1\frac{2}{5}$

d) $2\frac{5}{7} - 1\frac{1}{2}$ e) $2\frac{3}{5} - 1\frac{1}{4}$ f) $1\frac{2}{3} + 2\frac{2}{5}$

g) $2\frac{5}{7} - 1\frac{3}{4}$ h) $3\frac{7}{8} - 2\frac{1}{4}$ i) $1\frac{1}{6} + 3\frac{1}{4}$

EXERCISE 3.3

1 Work out the following. Give your answer as a fraction in its simplest form:

a) $\frac{3}{4} \times \frac{2}{5}$ b) $\frac{2}{3} \times \frac{5}{7}$ c) $\frac{1}{7} \times \frac{1}{4}$ d) $\frac{5}{8} \times \frac{3}{7}$ e) $\frac{2}{9} \times \frac{4}{5}$ f) $\frac{3}{11} \times \frac{4}{9}$

2 Work out the following. Give your answer as a fraction in its simplest form:

a) $\frac{3}{7} \div \frac{9}{10}$ b) $\frac{3}{5} \div \frac{6}{7}$ c) $\frac{2}{9} \div \frac{4}{7}$ d) $\frac{2}{3} \div \frac{8}{11}$ e) $\frac{5}{6} \div \frac{10}{17}$ f) $\frac{8}{9} \div \frac{9}{8}$

3 Work out the following. Give your answer as a fraction in its simplest form:

a) $\frac{1}{5} \times \frac{10}{11}$ b) $\frac{3}{7} \times \frac{5}{6}$ c) $\frac{9}{10} \div \frac{18}{7}$ d) $\frac{1}{3} \div \frac{5}{6}$ e) $\frac{5}{7} \times \frac{14}{15}$ f) $\frac{1}{8} \div \frac{1}{7}$

g) $\frac{1}{4} \div \frac{3}{10}$ h) $\frac{6}{35} \times \frac{14}{9}$ i) $\frac{4}{5} \times \frac{5}{6}$ j) $\frac{4}{5} \div \frac{5}{6}$ k) $\frac{1}{5} \times \frac{5}{6} \div \frac{1}{3}$ l) $\frac{1}{5} \times \frac{1}{3} \div \frac{5}{6}$

EXERCISE 3.4

Do not use your calculator for Questions 1–3.

1 Work out:

a) $\frac{1}{4}$ of 28   b) $\frac{1}{2}$ of 46   c) $\frac{1}{3}$ of 12

d) $\frac{1}{10}$ of 90   e) $\frac{1}{7}$ of 21   f) $\frac{1}{5}$ of 555

2 Work out:

a) $\frac{2}{3}$ of 21   b) $\frac{3}{4}$ of 40   c) $\frac{5}{7}$ of 35   d) $\frac{3}{5}$ of 30   e) $\frac{4}{11}$ of 88

f) $\frac{7}{9}$ of 63   g) $\frac{7}{10}$ of 60   h) $\frac{5}{6}$ of 24   i) $\frac{3}{8}$ of 32

3 At Southvale School $\frac{13}{20}$ of the students are female.

There are 1200 students at the school.
a) How many students are female?
b) What fraction of the students is male?
c) How many students are male?

You can use your calculator for Questions 4–6.

4

CECIL'S CYCLES
$\frac{1}{5}$ off
Normal price £380

BILLY'S BICYCLES
$\frac{2}{7}$ off
Normal price £420

Which bicycle is the cheapest? Show all your working.

5 A book normally costs £23.80
a) How much does it cost in the sale?

Henry buys a book for £12
b) What is the normal price of the book?

> **BOOK SALE**
> $\frac{1}{4}$ off all normal prices

6 A pair of rollerblades normally costs £56
a) How much does it cost in the sale?

Jan buys a pair of rollerblades for £30
b) What is the normal price of the rollerblades?

> *Rollerblade Sale*
> $\frac{2}{5}$ off all normal prices

EXERCISE 3.5

1 Write down the reciprocal of:
a) 3 **b)** 5 **c)** 9 **d)** 0.5
e) 0.125 **f)** $\frac{1}{7}$ **g)** $\frac{5}{8}$ **h)** $\frac{2}{3}$

2 a) Write down the reciprocal of:

(i) 5 **(ii)** 0.4 **(iii)** $\frac{7}{11}$

b) Write down the reciprocal of each of your answers to **a)**. What do you notice?

3 a) Multiply each number in question **1** by its reciprocal.
b) What do you notice?

U3 CHAPTER 4

Percentages

EXERCISE 4.1

Do not use your calculator for Questions 1–3.

1 A school has 300 students in each of Years 9, 10 and 11
The number of girls in each year group are:

      120 girls in Year 9
      210 girls in Year 10
      150 girls in Year 11

Write each of these as a percentage of the number of students in that year.

2 Maria buys a house for £240 000 and sells it three years later for £300 000
  a) How much profit has she made?
  b) What is her percentage profit?

3 Harry buys a book for £40 and sells it for £32
  a) How much money has he lost?
  b) What is his percentage loss?

You can use your calculator for Questions 4 and 5.

4 Jasmine gets these marks in her end of term tests.

  a) Write each of Jasmine's marks as a percentage.
  b) In which subject did she get her worst mark?
  c) In which subject did she get her best mark?

Subject	Mark
Business Studies	$\frac{22}{40}$
French	$\frac{36}{60}$
Maths	$\frac{93}{150}$
Religious Studies	$\frac{12}{30}$
Science	$\frac{132}{200}$
Spanish	$\frac{26}{50}$

5 Pete bought some items on the internet and then sold them at a garage sale.
What percentage profit or loss has he made on each of these items?
  a) Necklace bought for £240, sold for £360
  b) Boots bought for £60, sold for £45
  c) Painting bought for £500, sold for £380
  d) A CD collection bought for £80, sold for £90

EXERCISE 4.2

Do not use your calculator for Questions 1–3.

1 A choir had 50 members in January.
By the next December its membership had increased by 24%
How many members did the choir have in December?

2 Sheila went on a 3-month cruise.
She weighed 74 kg at the start of the cruise.
By the end of the cruise her weight had increased by 12%
Work out how much Sheila weighed at the end of the cruise.

3 Scott invested £2300 at 3% simple interest for one year.
How much does he have after one year?

You can use your calculator for Questions 4–6.

4 In a sale all items are reduced by 14%
What is the sale price for each of the following items?

Item	Price before the sale
Widescreen televisions	£800
DVD players	£64
Computers	£1200
Laptops	£950

5 Simon's restaurant bill is £64 plus a service charge of 12.5%
How much must Simon pay?

6 Matt invests £7800 at 2.5% simple interest for one year.
How much does he have after one year?

EXERCISE 4.3 (Extension Exercise)

1 Lily invests £6000 at 4% compound interest.
How much does she have after: **a)** 1 year **b)** 2 years **c)** 3 years?

2 A £23 000 car depreciates by 15% every year.
So its value **decreases** by 15% every year.
How much is the car worth after: **a)** 1 year **b)** 2 years **c)** 3 years?

3 Myra invests £8000 at 6% compound interest.
How much does she have after 3 years?

4 The value of a painting in an art gallery has increased by 20% each year for the last 4 years.
It was worth £53 000, 4 years ago.
How much is it worth today?
Give your answer to the nearest thousand pounds.

U3 CHAPTER 5

Expressions and formulae

EXERCISE 5.1

Do not use your calculator for Questions 1 and 2.

1 Use the formulae:

   area = base × perpendicular height
   perimeter = 2 × base + 2 × length of sloping side

   to work out the area and perimeter of these parallelograms:

a)

b)

c)

2 Use the formula $T = H \times R$, where T is the total pay, H is the number of hours worked, and R is the hourly rate, to work out the total pay for the following people:
   a) June works 20 hours and is paid £9 per hour
   b) Marvin is paid an hourly rate of £5 and he works for 70 hours
   c) Fahir's hourly rate of pay is £6 and he works for 12 hours
   d) Beth only works for 90 minutes but her hourly rate is £22 per hour.

You can use your calculator for Questions 3–5.

3 A caterer uses the following formula to work out their customers' bills.

Total bill (in £)	=	Standard charge	+	number of people at the dinner × £23	+	number of helpers needed × £50

Jasmine had 16 people for dinner and needed 3 helpers. The standard charge was £40
   a) How much does Jasmine have to pay the caterer?

Mike had a large birthday party. There were 100 people at the party and 8 helpers were needed. The standard charge was £40
   b) Work out Mike's total bill.

4 The speed of a car is given by the formula:
   $S = D \div T$

   Find the exact value of S when:
   a) $D = 540$ and $T = 18$ **b)** $D = 2142$ and $T = 34$
   c) $D = 1288$ and $T = 23$ **d)** $D = 302.4$ and $T = 3.6$

5 The area, A, of a trapezium is found using the formula:

$$A = \frac{p + q}{2} \times h$$

where p and q are the lengths of the parallel sides and h is the perpendicular height.

Find A when:
a) $p = 5, q = 7$ and $h = 6$
b) $p = 6, q = 8$ and $h = 2$
c) $p = 12, q = 18$ and $h = 5$
d) $p = 10, q = 5$ and $h = 3.6$

EXERCISE 5.2

Do not use your calculator for Questions 1–3.

1 When $p = 2, q = 6, r = 0$ and $t = 3$ find the value of:
a) $t + 6$ **b)** $8 - p$ **c)** $5q$ **d)** $4p - t$
e) $8r + q + p$ **f)** $7p + t$ **g)** q^2 **h)** pq
i) $2.5p + 6t$ **j)** ptr **k)** q^p **l)** t^3

2 When $x = 3, y = 8$ and $z = 4$ find the value of:
a) $5(x + z)$ **b)** $(2z)^2$ **c)** $2z^2$
d) $x(y - z)$ **e)** $10y^2$ **f)** $z(2y - 2x)$
g) $\dfrac{2y}{z}$ **h)** $(x + y)^2$ **i)** $\dfrac{x + y + z}{5}$

3 When $a = 9, b = 5$ and $c = -2$ find the value of:
a) $b + c$ **b)** $a + b^2$ **c)** $c^2 + b$
d) $\dfrac{a + b}{c}$ **e)** $\dfrac{b - c}{a - 2}$ **f)** $\dfrac{2a}{b + c}$

You can use your calculator for Questions 4–8.

4 When $c = 5, h = 7$ and $n = 3$, find the value of:
a) $2h - 3n$ **b)** $c^2 - 5n$ **c)** $ch - 2hn$ **d)** $(3c - 2h)^2$

5 When $e = 2, f = 4$ and $g = -3$, find the value of:
a) $(e + f)^2$ **b)** $3g + 2ef$ **c)** $2f - g$ **d)** $(3e - g)^2$

6 When $x = -6, y = -1$ and $z = 9$, find the value of:
a) $y^2 + 2z$ **b)** $xy + 2$ **c)** $5(y + x)$ **d)** $z(x - 10y)$ **e)** $5y^8$
f) $2x^2$ **g)** $(z + x)^3$ **h)** $7(2x + 3z)$ **i)** $\dfrac{x + 2z}{2y}$ **j)** $\dfrac{x^2}{yz}$

7 The velocity, v, of a particle is found using the formula:

$$v = u + at$$

where u is the initial velocity, t is the time and a is the acceleration.
   a) Use your calculator to work out the value of v when $a = 9.8$, $t = 3.57$ and $u = 2.43$
       Write down all the figures on your calculator display.
   b) Round your answer to part **a)** correct to 3 significant figures.

8 The distance, s, travelled by a particle is given by the formula:

$$s = ut + \tfrac{1}{2}at^2$$

where u is the initial velocity, t is the time and a is the acceleration.
   a) Use your calculator to work out the value of s when $a = 8.5$, $t = 6.5$ and $u = 1.7$
       Write down all the figures on your calculator display.
   b) Round your answer to part **a)** correct to an appropriate degree of accuracy.

EXERCISE 5.3

1 A triangle has sides of length x cm, $3y$ cm and $5z$ cm
   Write down a formula for the perimeter P of the triangle.

2 A square has length g cm
   Write down a formula in terms of g for:
   a) the perimeter P, of the square
   b) the area A, of the square.

3 A rectangle has width x cm
   Its length is 10 cm more than its width.
   Write down a formula in terms of x for:
   a) the length, L, of the rectangle
   b) the perimeter, P, of the rectangle
   c) the area, A, of the rectangle.

4 Becky buys n books at £p each.
   Obtain an equation for the total cost, C, for the books that Becky buys.

5 Pens cost 5p each and pencils cost 8p each.
   a) Nick buys x pens and y pencils.
       Write down an expression in terms of x and y for the total cost of the pens and
       pencils Nick buys.
   b) If the total cost is z pounds, write down an equation in terms of x, y and z

6 The cost of hiring a machine is £20 plus a daily charge of £5 per day.
   a) Find the cost of hiring the machine for 6 days.
   b) Obtain a formula for the cost, £C, of hiring the machine for x days.

7 In a school there are g girls and b boys.
  a) Write an expression for the total number of students in the school.
  b) Write a formula for the total number of students, N, in the school.

8 On Monday Melissa runs at p km/h for q hours.
  Write down a formula for the total distance, D, that Melissa runs on Monday.

EXERCISE 5.4

1 Rearrange these formulae to make a the subject:
  a) $b = a - 5$
  b) $c = 4 + a$
  c) $e = \dfrac{a}{2}$
  d) $f = 6a$
  e) $g = 9 - a$
  f) $h = \dfrac{1}{2}a$

2 Rearrange these formulae to make x the subject:
  a) $y = 3x - 4$
  b) $y = 5 + 2x$
  c) $y = \dfrac{x}{7} - 1$
  d) $y = 8 + \dfrac{x}{5}$
  e) $y = 6x + 1$
  f) $y = \dfrac{x - 1}{7}$

3 Rearrange these formulae to make w the subject:
  a) $y = wx$
  b) $y = w + v$
  c) $y = \dfrac{w}{c}$
  d) $y = 3w - c$
  e) $y = wh + 2e$
  f) $y = \dfrac{c}{w}$

4 Rearrange these formulae so that the indicated letter becomes the subject:
  a) $A = lw$ (w)
  b) $P = 2b + 2h$ (h)
  c) $y = 5x - 2$ (x)
  d) $D = s \times t$ (t)
  e) $E = \dfrac{360}{n}$ (n)
  f) $S = 180(n - 2)$ (n)
  g) $C = \pi d$ (d)
  h) $T = x(y - z)$ (x)
  i) $v = u + at$ (t)
  j) $m = \dfrac{y}{x}$ (y)

EXERCISE 5.5

1 Simplify:
  a) $a \times a \times a \times a$
  b) $b \times b \times b$
  c) $c \times c \times c \times c \times c$
  d) $7 \times e \times e$
  e) $8 \times f \times f \times f \times f$
  f) $4 \times g \times 2 \times g$

2 Simplify:
  a) $x^4 \times x^7$
  b) $x^3 \times x$
  c) $y^5 \times y^2$
  d) $c^{30} \div c^5$
  e) $d^{10} \div d^5$
  f) $z^5 \times z \times z^3$
  g) $y^{12} \div y^4$
  h) $e^3 \times e^3$
  i) $f^6 \div f$
  j) $g^{20} \div g^5$
  k) $h^6 \times h^3$
  l) $k^{10} \times k^2$

3 Simplify:
a) $7x^5 \times 2x^6$
b) $6x^3 \times 3x^3$
c) $8x^2 \times x^5$
d) $5x^5 \times 8x^4$
e) $9y \times 4y^7$
f) $3x^3 \times 3x^3$
g) $4x^2 \times 5x^6$
h) $3x^5 \times 4x^3 \times 2x$
i) $7x^3 \times x^9 \times 6x^5$

4 Simplify:
a) $15y^8 \div 3y^2$
b) $21z^7 \div 7z^3$
c) $63x^8 \div 7x^4$
d) $56z^3 \div 8z$
e) $80y^{10} \div 8y^5$
f) $16y^6 \div 16y^4$
g) $13x^7 \div 13x^7$
h) $18x^{18} \div 2x^2$
i) $15x^5 \div 3x^3$

EXERCISE 5.6

1 Which of the following statements are correct?
a) $2x + 3x \equiv 4x + x$
b) $5 - 9x \equiv -4x$
c) $7x - 3x \equiv x + 3x$
d) $2(x + 3) \equiv 2x + 3$

2 Which of the following expressions are always equal to $4n$?

| $6n - 2$ | $9n - 5n$ | $n \times 4$ | $4(n + 1) - 4$ | $2n \times 2n$ | $n + 3n$ |

3 a) Show that when $x = 5$, $(x - 2)^2 = x^2 - 4x + 4$
   b) By expanding $(x - 2)^2$ show that you can write $(x - 2)^2 \equiv x^2 - 4x + 4$

U3 CHAPTER 6

Equations

EXERCISE 6.1

Look at the various algebraic statements labelled **A** to **J**:

A $7x + 2 = 3$ **B** $6y + 5$

C πr^2 **D** $V = L \times B \times H$

E $5x - 2x = 3x$ **F** $x^3 = 27$

G $2c + 3 = c + 3 + c$ **H** $A = \frac{1}{2}(a + b)h$

I $x^2 - 9$ **J** $12x = 30$

1 Which statements are expressions?

2 Which statements are equations?

3 Which statements would you call formulae?

4 Which statements are identities?

EXERCISE 6.2

Do not use your calculator for Questions 1–4.

Show all your working when answering the questions in this exercise.

1 Solve:
   a) $a + 7 = 10$ **b)** $b - 3 = 18$ **c)** $c + 11 = 24$

2 Solve:
   a) $a - 7 = 7$ **b)** $b + 15 = 35$ **c)** $c - 20 = 55$

3 Solve:
   a) $3a = 21$ **b)** $\dfrac{b}{5} = 4$ **c)** $9c = 18$

4 Solve:
   a) $\dfrac{a}{2} = 7$ **b)** $\dfrac{b}{6} = 5$ **c)** $8c = 24$

You can use your calculator for Questions 5 and 6.

5 Solve:
   a) $x + 5 = 27$ **b)** $x - 18 = 7$ **c)** $6x = 54$

   d) $\frac{1}{2}x = 8$ **e)** $x - 13 = 44$ **f)** $\dfrac{x}{4} = 15$

   g) $5x = 80$ **h)** $\dfrac{x}{7} = 21$ **i)** $x + 42 = 42$

6 Solve:

  a) $8t = 48$

  b) $u - 6 = 4$

  c) $\frac{1}{4}p = 5$

  d) $20g = 10$

  e) $5q = 1$

  f) $w + 8 = 3$

  g) $6y = 5$

  h) $y + 12 = 5$

  i) $\frac{p}{6} = -3$

EXERCISE 6.3

Do not use your calculator for Questions 1 and 2.

1 Solve:

  a) $2a + 7 = 15$ **b)** $4b - 1 = 7$ **c)** $9c + 5 = 23$

  d) $5 + 3d = 20$ **e)** $7e - 3 = 4$ **f)** $6f + 13 = 31$

  g) $5g + 3 = 3$ **h)** $1 + 8h = 41$ **i)** $10i - 10 = 10$

2 Solve:

  a) $7 - a = 3$ **b)** $15 - b = 10$ **c)** $20 - c = 14$

  d) $9 - 2d = 5$ **e)** $11 - 3e = 2$ **f)** $8 - 4f = 0$

  g) $25 - 7g = 4$ **h)** $30 - 6h = 0$ **i)** $6 - 2i = 4$

You can use your calculator for Questions 3 and 4.

3 Solve:

  a) $5a + 7 = 17$ **b)** $2b - 1 = 15$ **c)** $3c + 2 = 14$

  d) $9 + 7d = 23$ **e)** $6e - 5 = 25$ **f)** $27 + 4f = 3$

  g) $8g - 3 = -27$ **h)** $9h + 11 = 2$ **i)** $10i - 3 = 7$

4 Solve:

  a) $\dfrac{a + 3}{2} = 4$

  b) $\dfrac{b - 7}{3} = 5$

  c) $\dfrac{2c}{5} - 1 = 3$

  d) $\dfrac{9 + d}{4} = 2$

  e) $\dfrac{3e}{7} + 1 = 4$

  f) $\dfrac{2 - f}{3} = 1$

  g) $\dfrac{g - 4}{5} = 3$

  h) $\dfrac{2 - 3h}{7} = 5$

  i) $12 - \dfrac{i}{8} = 4$

EXERCISE 6.4

Solve:

1 $5(a + 2) = 20$ **2** $6(2b - 1) = 12$ **3** $4(3c + 4) = 16$

4 $2(5 - d) = 6$ **5** $9(4e + 1) = 45$ **6** $3(20 - f) = 21$

7 $7(2g - 3) = 70$ **8** $8(6 + 5h) = 144$ **9** $5(6i + 1) = 35$

10 $3(9 + 4j) = 33$ **11** $6(3k - 7) = 30$ **12** $4(2l - 1) = -20$

EXERCISE 6.5

Solve these algebraic equations, showing the steps of your working clearly.
All the answers are integers, but some may be negative.

1 $3x + 2 = x + 12$ **2** $22 + 5x = 6x$

3 $9x + 4 = 4x + 29$ **4** $x + 5 = 13 - x$

5 $8x + 3 = 48 - x$ **6** $23 - 2x = 33 - 7x$

7 $5x + 3 = 15 - x$ **8** $7 + 4x = 2x + 9$

9 $8x - 5 = x + 9$ **10** $6x = 42 - x$

Expand any brackets and simplify before solving these equations.

11 $6(x - 3) + 2 = 14$ **12** $3(x - 4) = 23 - 2x$

13 $4(x + 10) = 50 - x$ **14** $8(x - 3) = 8$

15 $2(5x + 3) = 7x + 24$ **16** $x + 7 = 5(x - 1)$

17 $4(3x - 5) = 3(2x + 1) + 1$ **18** $5(x - 1) = 3(x - 5)$

19 $7(x + 8) = 4(x + 7) - 14$ **20** $2(5x + 3) = 4(x - 3)$

EXERCISE 6.6

Do not use your calculator for Questions 1–6.

1 A CD costs £5. Tim buys x CDs.
   a) Write down an expression, in terms of x, for the total cost of Tim's CDs.
   Tim spends £80 on CDs.
   b) Write down an equation to show this information.
   c) Solve your equation to find how many CDs Tim buys.

2 A rectangle has length $(c + 8)$ cm and width c cm
   a) Write down an expression, in terms of c, for the
      perimeter of the rectangle.
   The perimeter of the rectangle is 60 cm
   b) Write down an equation to show this information.
   c) Solve your equation to find the width and length of the rectangle.

3 Ben earned y euros per hour in January.
In February his earnings were increased by 2 euros per hour.
  a) Write down an expression, in terms of y, for Ben's new earnings per hour.
  b) Write down an expression, using brackets, if Ben works for 10 hours in February.

Ben earns 170 euros in February for 10 hours' work.
  c) Write down an equation for this information.
  d) Solve your equation to find the value of y

4

I think of a number.
I add 7 to my number and
then multiply this by 5
The answer is 20

Seyi

I think of a number.
I divide my number by 10 and
then add 16 to the result.
The answer is 36

Jamie

  a) (i) Use x to stand for Seyi's mystery number.
           Write down an equation for Seyi's mystery number.
      (ii) Solve your equation to find Seyi's number.
  b) Use y to stand for Jamie's mystery number.
      (i) Write down an equation for Jamie's mystery number.
      (ii) Solve your equation to find Jamie's number.

5 An isosceles triangle has two sides of length x cm
The third side is 4 cm more than each of the other two sides.
  a) Write down an expression for the third side of the triangle.
  b) (i) Write down an expression for the perimeter
           of the triangle.
      (ii) Simplify your expression.
The perimeter of the triangle is 40 cm

  c) Work out the lengths of all three sides of the triangle.

6 A triangle has angles of $x + 30°, 2x + 10°$ and $x + 20°$

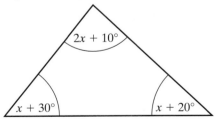

  a) Write down an expression, in terms of x, for the sum of the 3 angles.
  b) (i) Use the fact that the angles of a triangle add up to $180°$ to write an equation in
           terms of x
      (ii) Solve your equation to find the value of x
  c) Write down the size of the biggest angle.

You can use your calculator for Questions 7–10.

7 a) Write down an expression for the area of this square.

The area of the square is 225 cm^2

t cm

b) What is the length of one side of the square?

8 a) (i) Write down an expression in terms of x for the perimeter of this rectangle.

(ii) Simplify your expression.

$5x - 2$

$2x + 5$
(width)

b) (i) Write down an expression in terms of x for the perimeter of this triangle.

$x + 12$ $x + 12$

$3x$

(ii) Simplify your expression.

The perimeter of the rectangle is the same as the perimeter of the triangle.
All measurements are in cm

c) (i) Write down an equation to show this information.

(ii) Solve your equation to find the width of the rectangle.

9 a) Write down an expression for this information.
Use n for Marco's mystery number.

I think of a number.
I multiply the number by 7
I then add 5 to the new total.

Marco

Marco gets the same answer when he adds 29 to his mystery number.

b) Write down an equation for this information.

c) Solve your equation to find Marco's mystery number.

10 Michael and Tanya each think of the same number.
Michael multiplies the number by 4, and then adds 2
Tanya adds 4 to the number, and then multiplies the answer by 2
They both end up with the same answer.

a) Write this information as an equation.

b) Solve your equation to find the number they both thought of.

EXERCISE 6.7

Use trial and improvement to solve these equations correct to 1 decimal place.

1 The equation $x^2 + 3x = 24$ has a solution between $x = 3$ and $x = 4$

2 The equation $x^2 + x = 33$ has a solution between $x = 5$ and $x = 6$

3 The equation $x^3 + x = 4$ has a solution between $x = 1$ and $x = 2$

4 The equation $x^2 - 5x = 20$ has a solution between $x = 7$ and $x = 8$

5 The equation $x^3 + 7 = 100$ has a solution between $x = 4$ and $x = 5$

6 The equation $x^2 - 5 = 70$ has a solution between $x = 8$ and $x = 9$

7 The equation $2x^2 + x = 2$ has a solution between $x = 0$ and $x = 1$

Use trial and improvement to solve these equations correct to 2 decimal places.

8 The equation $2x^3 - x = 500$ has a solution between $x = 6$ and $x = 7$

9 The equation $x^2(x + 1) = 34$ has a solution between 2 and 3

10 The equation $x^2 + 2x = 7$ has a solution between $x = 1$ and $x = 2$

EXERCISE 6.8

1 Write down the correct inequality sign ($<$ or $>$) between these pairs of numbers:
  a) 6 ... 9
  b) 3.7 ... 2.9
  c) 6 ... 5.97
  d) 3.08 ... 3.8
  e) -5 ... -6
  f) -9 ... 0
  g) -22 ... -20
  h) -6.8 ... -6.9
  i) 20 ... -18

2 Show these inequalities on a number line:
  a) $a \leqslant 2$
  b) $b > -1$
  c) $c \geqslant 5$
  d) $-4 < d < 3$
  e) $-2 \leqslant e \leqslant 3$
  f) $-5 < f \leqslant -1$

3 Write down the possible integer values for x:
  a) $2 < x < 8$
  b) $-3 \leqslant x \leqslant 1$
  c) $1 < x \leqslant 6$
  d) $-5 \leqslant x < 0$
  e) $-8 < x < -3$
  f) $-4 < x \leqslant 2$

4 Solve these inequalities:
  a) $y + 5 \leqslant 9$
  b) $y - 2 \geqslant 3$
  c) $7y > 21$
  d) $5y < 30$
  e) $2y - 3 \geqslant 5$
  f) $7 + 4y \leqslant 27$

5 Solve these inequalities:
  a) $4 \leqslant x + 2 \leqslant 12$
  b) $-2 \leqslant x - 6 < 3$
  c) $-9 < 3x < 24$
  d) $35 < 5x \leqslant 50$
  e) $6 < x - 3 \leqslant 15$
  f) $-8 \leqslant 2x \leqslant -2$

6 Write down the possible integer values for n:
  a) $5 \leqslant n + 1 \leqslant 8$
  b) $4 \leqslant 2n < 16$
  c) $-6 \leqslant 3n \leqslant 12$
  d) $7 < n - 3 < 12$
  e) $-5 < n + 2 \leqslant -2$
  f) $-30 \leqslant 5n < -10$

U3 CHAPTER 7

Graphs

 EXERCISE 7.1

Find the gradient of the lines marked in Questions **1–6** below.

1

2

3

4

5

6

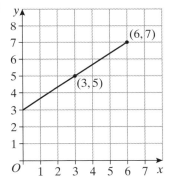

7 Find the gradient of the line joining the points $(5, 3)$ and $(15, 7)$

8 Find the gradient of the line joining the points $(9, 12)$ and $(15, 0)$

EXERCISE 7.2

1 Write down the gradients of the lines:

   a) $y = 6x$ **b)** $y = \frac{1}{3}x$ **c)** $y = 2x - 7$

   d) $y = -3x$ **e)** $y = 8 - 5x$ **f)** $y = x + 2$

2 The diagram shows the graph
   corresponding to a linear function of x
   a) Write down the coordinates of the points P and Q on
   the line.
   b) Write down the gradient and
   the y intercept of the line.
   c) Hence find the equation of the
   straight line.

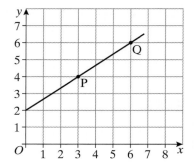

3 The diagram shows the graph of a
   linear function of x
   a) Find the gradient and the y intercept
   of the line.
   b) Hence write down the equation of the
   straight line.

EXERCISE 7.3

1 a) On the same axes draw the graphs of:
   $y = 3x - 1$ and $y = 2x$
   b) Write down the coordinates of the point of intersection.
   c) Hence solve the simultaneous equations:
   $y = 3x - 1$
   $y = 2x$

2 a) On the same axes draw the graphs of:
   $y = 4$ and $y = 4x$
   b) Write down the coordinates of the point of intersection.
   c) Hence solve the simultaneous equations:
   $y = 4$
   $y = 4x$

3 a) On the same axes draw the graphs of:
   $y = 3x$ and $y = x + 2$
   b) Write down the coordinates of the point of intersection.
   c) Hence solve the simultaneous equations:
   $y = 3x$
   $y = x + 2$

4 a) On the same axes draw the graphs of:
$y = x + 1$ and $x + y = 7$
b) Write down the coordinates of the point of intersection.
c) Hence solve the simultaneous equations:
$y = x + 1$
$x + y = 7$

5 a) On the same axes draw the graphs of:
$y = x - 3$ and $x = 4$
b) Write down the coordinates of the point of intersection.
c) Hence solve the simultaneous equations:
$y = x - 3$
$x = 4$

EXERCISE 7.4

1 a) Complete a copy of the table of values for $y = x^2 + 1$

x	-3	-2	-1	0	1	2	3
x^2	9		1			4	
$+1$	$+1$		$+1$			$+1$	
y	10		2			5	

b) Draw the graph of $y = x^2 + 1$

2 a) Complete a copy of the table of values for $y = x^2 - 2$

x	-4	-3	-2	-1	0	1	2	3	4
x^2	16			1	0	1		9	
-2	-2			-2		-2		-2	
y	14			-1				7	

b) Draw the graph of $y = x^2 - 2$
c) Use your graph to solve the equation $x^2 - 2 = 0$

3 a) Complete a copy of the table of values for $y = 2x^2$

x	-4	-3	-2	-1	0	1	2	3	4
x^2		9			0		4		
y		18					8		

b) Draw the graph of $y = 2x^2$

4 a) Complete a copy of the table of values for $y = 2x^2 + 3$

x	-4	-3	-2	-1	0	1	2	3	4
x^2		9					4		
$2x^2$		18					8		
$+3$		$+3$					$+3$		
y		21					11		

b) Draw the graph of $y = 2x^2 + 3$

5 a) Complete a copy of the table of values for $y = x^2 - x - 5$

x	-4	-3	-2	-1	0	1	2	3	4
x^2	16	9						9	
$-x$	$+4$	$+3$						-3	
-5	-5	-5						-5	
y	15	7						1	

b) Draw the graph of $y = x^2 - x - 5$
c) Use your graph to solve the equation $x^2 - x + 5 = 0$

6 Draw the following graphs for $-3 \leqslant x \leqslant 3$:
a) $y = 3x^2$ **b)** $y = x^2 - 5$ **c)** $y = 2x^2 - 2$
d) $y = x^2 - x$ **e)** $y = 2x^2 - 2x$ **f)** $y = x^2 + 2x - 2$

EXERCISE 7.5

1 This conversion graph converts between pounds (lb) and kilograms (kg).
  a) A new-born baby weighs 8 lbs
    What is the baby's weight in kg?
  b) A bag of potatoes weighs 5 kg
    What is the weight of the
    bag of potatoes in lbs?
  c) Barbara buys some chocolate
    for her bakery.
    The chocolate in Box A weighs 18 lbs
    The chocolate in Box B weighs 8.4 kg
    Both boxes cost the same.
    Which is the better buy?
    Give reasons for your answer.

2 The graph shows Jean's weight during the first 12 weeks of her diet.

a) How much did Jean weigh at the start of her diet?
b) How much did Jean weigh after: **(i)** 2 weeks   **(ii)** 5 weeks?
c) How long did it take for Jean to lose 20 kg?

3 Water runs out of a hole in the bottom of a container.
The water runs out at a steady rate.
The diagram below shows how the depth of water in the container varies over time.

A   **B**   **C**

Say which container, A, B or C, best matches this graph.
Explain your reasoning.

4 Water is poured into a container at a constant
rate. The container is in the shape of a cone,
as shown in the diagram.
Sketch a set of depth/time axes, and complete
the diagram to show how the depth of water in
the container changes over time.

EXERCISE 7.6

Do not use your calculator for Questions 1–3.

1 Uzma cycles to her friend's house.
Here is a description of her journey:

- Uzma leaves her house at 8 am.
- She cycles 10 km to arrive at her friend's house at 9.30 am.
- Uzma spends 75 minutes with her friend.
- Uzma then cycles back towards her home but stops after 4 km, at 11.15 am to have a rest.
- She rests for $\frac{1}{4}$ hour.
- She then cycles straight home, arriving at 12.30 pm.

a) Draw a travel graph of Uzma's journey.
b) What is Uzma's average speed, in km per hour, on her way to her friend's house?

2 Every morning Ivan walks to school and walks home after school.
The travel graph shows his journey to school and his stay at school one Friday.

a) What time does Ivan arrive at his school on Friday?
b) How long does Ivan stay at school on Friday?

After school, Ivan walks slowly home at a constant speed. But on Friday he stops after half an hour to visit his friend who lives 1 km from school.
He stays at his friend's house for an hour and then continues walking home at a constant speed.
He arrives home at 6 pm.

c) Copy and complete the travel graph for Ivan's journey.
d) What is Ivan's average speed, in km per hour, on the way to school?

3 One Saturday Maya drives from Liverpool to Manchester to visit her grandmother. She stops along the way to get some flowers.
On her way home she stops for petrol and a coffee before returning to Liverpool.
The travel graph shows her journey.

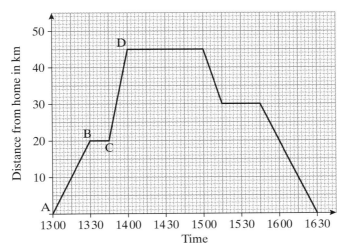

a) How long does Maya stop for flowers?
b) What time does Maya get to her grandmother's house?
c) How far is her grandmother from Maya's house?
d) How long did Maya stop for petrol and coffee?
e) Is Maya's speed greater between A and B or between C and D?
   Explain how you can tell.
f) What time does Maya arrive home?

You can use your calculator for Questions 4–9.

4 Claire leaves her house for school at 7 am each morning.
She walks to the bus stop and waits for her bus.
Here is a distance–time graph for
Claire's journey to school.
a) What time does Claire reach the bus stop?
b) How long does she have to wait for
   the bus?
c) How far away from Claire's house is:
   (i) the bus stop
   (ii) the school?
d) What is Claire's average speed, in km per
   hour, on her journey:
   (i) from A to B
   (ii) from C to D?

5 One morning Jamie leaves Crantown to visit his girlfriend in Daly.
That same day Peter leaves Daly to visit his Aunt in Crantown.
Here is a travel graph of their journeys.

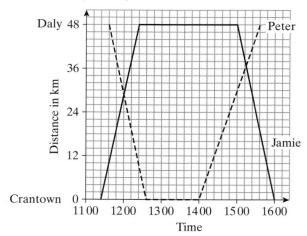

a) What is the distance between Crantown and Daly?
b) What time does Peter leave Daly?
c) What time does Jamie leave Crantown?
d) How far away from Crantown are they when they meet for the first time?
e) How long does Peter spend in Crantown?
f) What time do they meet on their journey home?

6 Geoff went by coach to Bradingham
Gardens for lunch.
The coach went directly to the
gardens from the coach stop.
On the way home the coach
stopped at a stall.
The travel graph below shows
Geoff's journey.

a) How long did Geoff spend at
Bradingham Gardens?
b) Work out the speed of the coach,
in miles per hour, on the
outward journey.
c) Did the coach travel at the same
speed as this on the **return**
journey?

7 The diagram shows a distance–time graph for a train travelling between Farham and Gradel.

The train leaves Farham at 14 00 for its outward journey to Gradel.

The train leaves Gradel at 16 40 for its return journey to Farham.

a) Work out the speed of the train on its journey from Gradel to Farham.
b) State one difference between the outward journey and the return journey.
c) State one thing that is the same on the outward journey and the return journey.

At 15 00 a second train leaves Gradel.
It travels towards Farham at a constant speed of 40 miles per hour.
d) On a copy of the graph, draw the journey of the second train.
e) At what time do the two trains pass each other?

8 A group of hikers are hiking from their camp to a ruined castle.
They set off from their camp at 08 00
They walk for 2 hours at 3 km per hour.
They stop for a 30 minute rest.
After the rest, they walk on for a further $2\frac{1}{2}$ hours at 4 km per hour.
Then they stop for lunch for 1 hour.
After lunch, they walk on for a further 2 hours at 4 km per hour until they reach the ruined castle.
a) On a copy of the grid, complete the travel graph.

b) How far is the ruined castle from the camp?

9 Zac climbs a steep hill.
He gains height at a rate of 5 metres per minute.
It takes him 1 hour to reach the top.
He then stops for 45 minutes to have lunch.
Then he climbs back down, at 10 metres per minute.
  a) How high is the hill?
  b) How long does Zac's descent take?
  c) Copy and complete the graph below, numbering the scales on both axes.

Time in minutes

U3 CHAPTER 8

Angles in polygons

EXERCISE 8.1

1 Find the value of y

2 Find the value of m

3 a) Write down an expression for the sum
of the angles in the triangle.
Simplify your expression.
  b) Write down an equation for the sum of the angles in the
triangle.
  c) Solve your equation to find the value of x
  d) Hence work out the value of each angle.

4 a) Write down an expression for the
sum of the angles in the triangle.
Simplify your expression.
  b) Write down an equation for the sum of the angles in the
triangle.
  c) Solve your equation to find the value of y
  d) Hence work out the value of each angle.

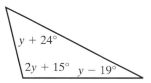

5 A triangle has angles $3x + 16°, 2x − 26°$ and $90°$
  a) Set up an equation in x
  b) Solve your equation to find the value of x
  c) Work out the size of the angles in the triangle.

6 The angles in a triangle are $2y + 10°, 6y − 32°$ and $4y + 10°$
  a) Set up an equation in y
  b) Solve your equation to find the value of y
  c) Work out the size of the angles in the triangle.

7 The diagram shows a quadrilateral.
Work out the value of g

8 The diagram shows a quadrilateral.
Work out the value of y

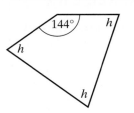

9 Find the size of the angles marked h

10 a) Form an equation in y
   b) Solve your equation to find y
   c) Hence find the size of the angles in the quadrilateral.

11 a) Form an equation in k
   b) Solve your equation to find k
   c) Hence find the size of the two angles on the straight line.

12 a) Set up an equation in x
   b) Solve your equation to find the value of x
   c) Work out the size of all four angles.
   d) Check that your four answers add up to $360°$

EXERCISE 8.2

1 a) Find the sum of the interior angles of:
   (i) a regular hexagon   **(ii)** a regular 10-sided polygon.
   b) Find the size of each interior angle of:
   (i) a regular hexagon   **(ii)** a regular 10-sided polygon.
   c) Do the following tessellate?
   (i) a regular hexagon   **(ii)** a regular 10-sided polygon
   Give a reason for each answer.

2 a) Work out the size of the exterior angle at each vertex of:
   (i) a regular pentagon   **(ii)** a regular 12-sided polygon.
b) Work out the size of the interior angle at each vertex of:
   (i) a regular pentagon   **(ii)** a regular 12-sided polygon.
c) Do the following tessellate:
   (i) regular pentagon   **(ii)** a regular 12-sided polygon?
   Give a reason for each answer.

3 Seven of the angles in an octagon are $152°, 123°, 168°, 145°, 110°, 125°$ and $130°$
Find the eighth angle.

4 a) The diagram shows part of a regular polygon.
Work out how many sides the polygon has.

Emma draws this diagram.
She says it shows part of a regular polygon.

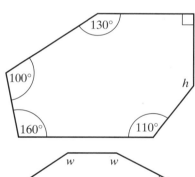

b) Explain how you can tell that Emma must have made a mistake.

5 The diagram shows an irregular hexagon.
Work out the value of h

6 The diagram shows an octagon.
All the angles marked w are equal.
Calculate the value of w

7 a) Write down an expression for the sum
of the angles in the pentagon.
Simplify your expression.
b) Write down an equation for the sum of the
angles in the pentagon.
c) Solve your equation to find the value of x
d) Hence work out the value of each angle.

8 Follow these instructions to make an accurate drawing of a regular pentagon.

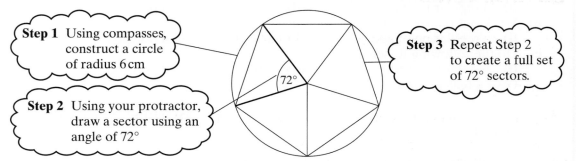

Step 1 Using compasses, construct a circle of radius 6 cm

Step 2 Using your protractor, draw a sector using an angle of 72°

72°

Step 3 Repeat Step 2 to create a full set of 72° sectors.

Complete the construction by joining the 5 points around the circumference of the circle.

9 Adapt the instructions from question **8** to make:
   a) a regular hexagon
   b) a regular 10-sided polygon
   c) a 10-pointed star.

U3 CHAPTER 9

Circles, cylinders and prisms

EXERCISE 9.1

Give the answers to each of these problems correct to 3 significant figures.

1 Find the circumference of these circles:

a)
•←5 cm→

b)
←12 mm→

c)
9 cm

d)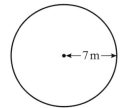
•←7 m→

2 Find the area of these circles:

a)
•←6 cm→

b)
←4 m→

c)
←1 cm→

d)
•←10 cm→

3 A circle has radius 11 mm
Find its circumference.

4 A circle has diameter 30 cm
Find its circumference.

5 A circle has radius 15 cm
Find its area.

6 A circle has diameter 42.8 cm
Find its area.

7 A circle has diameter 13 cm
Find its area.

8 A circle has radius 0.43 m
Find its area.

9 A circle has diameter 370 cm
Find its circumference.

10 A circle has radius 8.05 m
Find its circumference.

EXERCISE 9.2

Give the answers to each of these problems correct to 3 significant figures.

1. A circle has a diameter of 24 mm. Calculate its circumference.

2. A face of a coin is a circle of diameter of 32.4 mm. Calculate its area.

3. Anna decides to run around a circular race track.
   The radius of the track is 30 metres.
   a) Work out the length of one lap of the track.

   Anna wants to run at least 2000 metres.
   She wants to run a whole number of laps.
   b) Work out the minimum number of laps that Anna must run.

4. The diagram shows a rectangle inside a circle.
   The circle has a radius of 50 cm
   The rectangle measures 80 cm by 60 cm
   The corners of the rectangle are on the circumference of the circle.
   a) Work out the area of the rectangle.
   b) Work out the area of the circle.
   c) Work out the shaded area.
   Give your answer correct to the nearest square centimetre.

5. The diagram shows a rectangular piece of card with
   four circles cut out of it.
   The circles are each of diameter 5 cm
   The rectangle measures 24 cm by 13 cm
   a) Calculate the area of one of the circular holes.
   b) Work out the area of the card.

6. A circular table stands on a circular base.
   The diameter of the table top is 94 cm
   The radius of the base is 33 cm
   a) Calculate the area of the table top.
   b) Calculate the circumference of the base.

7. A bicycle wheel has a diameter of 70 cm
   a) How far, in metres, does the wheel go when it completes one revolution?
   b) How far, in metres, does the wheel go when it completes 20 revolutions?
   c) How many revolutions does the wheel complete when it travels 80 m?

8. The diagram shows a circular garden with a circular pond in the middle.
   The whole garden, apart from the pond, is lawn.
   The garden has a radius of 5 m
   The pond has a diameter of 2 m
   a) Calculate the area of the pond.
   b) Calculate the area of the garden.
   c) Hence find the area of the lawn.

   The gardener wants to put some fertiliser on the lawn.
   One bag of fertiliser is sufficient for 0.8 m²
   d) Work out how many bags of fertiliser the gardener needs to buy.

EXERCISE 9.3

Give the answers to each of these problems correct to 3 significant figures.

1 Calculate **(i)** the perimeter, **(ii)** the area of each sector.

a)

8 cm

b)

15 cm

c)

5 cm

d)

←3 cm→

e)

←7 cm→

f)

4.5 cm

g)

←2 cm→

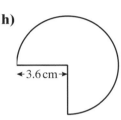

h)

←3.6 cm→

2 A pizza of diameter 16 inches is to be shared between two people.
The pizza is cut into two equal sectors.
Work out the area of pizza each person receives.

3 The diagram shows a running track at a school.
It is made up of two straight sections,
and two semicircular sections.
The dimensions are marked on the diagram.

40 m

48 m

100 m

Andy runs around the outside boundary of the
track, marked with a solid line.
Colin runs around the inside boundary, marked
with a dotted line.
They each run one lap of the track.
a) Work out how far Colin runs.
b) Work out how much further Andy runs than Colin.

4 Work out the total area of the shaded segments
in the diagram on the right.

6 cm

←6 cm→←6 cm→

EXERCISE 9.4

Give the answers to each of these problems correct to 3 significant figures.

1 A circle has circumference 46.7 cm
Find its diameter.

2 A circle has circumference 38.2 cm
Find its diameter.

3 A circle has circumference 55 m
Find its diameter.

4 A circle has circumference 28 mm
Find its radius.

5 A circle has circumference 39 cm
Find its radius.

6 A circle has circumference 18 m
Find its radius.

7 A circle has circumference 60 cm
Find its radius.

8 A circle has circumference 3 m
Find its radius.

9 The diagram shows a running track.
The ends are semicircles of radius y metres.
The straight sides are of length 45 metres each.
The total distance around the track
is 120 metres.

Calculate the value of y

EXERCISE 9.5

Give the answers to each of these problems correct to 3 significant figures.

1 A cylinder has radius 15 cm and height 23 cm
Find its volume.

2 A cylinder has radius 4 cm and height 3 cm
Find its curved surface area.

3 A cylinder has diameter 36 cm and height 10 cm
   a) Find its volume.
   b) Find its curved surface area.

4 A cylinder has radius 7 cm and height 18 cm
Find its volume.

5 The diagram on the right shows a hollow cylinder.
Work out the curved surface area of the cylinder.

6 A hollow cylindrical pipeline has an internal diameter of 16 cm
The pipeline is 250 metres in length.
   a) Work out the volume of the pipeline. Give your answer in cm^3
   b) 1000 cm^3 = 1 litre. Express the volume of the pipeline in litres.

7 A tube of crisps is in the shape of a cylinder.
It has radius 7 cm and height 30 cm
Work out the volume of the cylinder.

8 A sweet packet is in the shape of a hollow cardboard cylinder.
It has an inside diameter of 4.5 cm and a height of 12 cm
   a) Work out the volume of the cylinder.

The sweets have a volume of 2.3 cm^3 each.
   b) Show that the packet cannot contain 90 sweets.

9 Rosie wants to buy a can of soup.
She wants to buy the can of soup that
has the greatest volume.

Which of these two cans should she buy?
Show all your working.

A

B

EXERCISE 9.6

1 A circle has diameter 30 cm
Work out its **a)** circumference, **b)** area.
Leave your answers in terms of π

2 A circle has radius 18 cm
Work out its **a)** circumference, **b)** area.
Leave your answers in terms of π

3 A cylinder has radius 10 cm and
height 7 cm. Work out its:
a) curved surface area, **b)** volume.
Leave your answers in terms of π

4 A circle has circumference 39π cm
Work out **a)** the exact radius,
b) the exact area of the circle.
Leave your answers in terms of π

5 A circle has a circumference of 5π cm
  a) Work out the exact radius of the circle.
  b) Work out the exact area of the circle.
  Leave your answers in terms of π

6 A cylinder has volume 580π cm³
It has radius 20 cm.
Work out its height.

7 A cylinder has volume 360π cm³
It has radius 10 cm.
Work out its height.

8 The diagram shows a quadrant of a circle. The radius is 8 cm
  a) Work out the area of the quadrant, in terms of π
  b) Find an exact expression for the perimeter of this quadrant.

9 The diagram shows an unusual carpet.
It is in the shape of a square, with semicircles on each of
the four sides. The square is of side 20 m
  a) Work out the area of one of the semicircles.
    Leave your answer in terms of π
  b) Find an exact expression for the total area of the carpet.

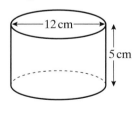

10 The diagram shows two cylinders.
Cylinder A has diameter 5 cm and height 12 cm
Cylinder B has diameter 12 cm and height 5 cm

Cylinder A   *Cylinder B*

  a) Show that both cylinders have exactly the same curved surface area.
  b) Work out the volume of each cylinder, leaving your answers in terms of π
  c) Which cylinder has the larger volume?

EXERCISE 9.7

Give your answers to an appropriate degree of accuracy.

1 Work out the volume of these prisms:

a)

1.2 m²   4 m

b)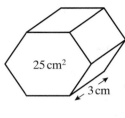

25 cm²   3 cm

c)

78 cm²   10 cm

2 Find **(i)** the volume, **(ii)** the surface area of these prisms:

a)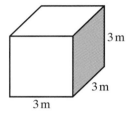

3 m   3 m   3 m

b)

8 cm   5 cm   10 cm

c)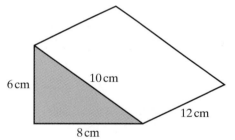

6 cm   10 cm   12 cm   8 cm

3 Look at this cuboid.
Tom has worked out:
A, the perimeter of the shaded face
B, the surface area
C, the volume.

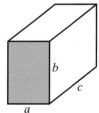

b   c   a

Here are his answers:

(i) | 12 cm | **(ii)** | 82 cm² | **(iii)** | 42 cm³ |

a) Match together A, B and C with Tom's answers.

Here are the formulae he used:

(i) | abc | **(ii)** | 2a + 2b | **(iii)** | 2ab + 2bc + 2ac |

b) Match together A, B and C with Tom's formulae.

4 The diagram shows a sketch of a swimming pool.

The pool is 1 m deep at the shallow end, and 3 m deep at the deep end.
The pool is 25 m long and 8 m wide.
a) Work out the volume of the pool.
   1 cubic metre = 1000 litres
b) Work out the number of litres of water in the pool when it is full.

5 A cube has a volume of 1000 cm^3
a) Work out the dimensions of the cube.
b) Calculate the surface area of the cube.

6 A cuboid has a volume of 40 cm^3
Its dimensions are all integers bigger than 1
No two dimensions are the same.
a) Work out the dimensions of the cuboid.
b) Calculate the surface area of the cuboid.

7 The diagram shows a water tank.
It is in the shape of a cuboid.
It has no lid.
a) Work out the volume of the tank, correct
   to 3 significant figures.
b) Work out the total surface area of the
   inside of the tank.

8 The cross section of a steel girder is in the shape of a letter T.
The cross section is shown in the diagram.
a) Work out the area of the T-shaped cross section.

The girder is 50 cm long.
b) Work out the volume of the girder.

EXERCISE 9.8

Change the following measurements:
a) 8100 cm^2 to m^2
b) 0.92 m^3 to cm^3
c) 3 m^3 to cm^3
d) 1.2 cm^3 to mm^3
e) 100 mm^3 to cm^3
f) 5 m^2 to cm^2
g) 0.07 m^3 to cm^3
h) 0.91 cm^3 to mm^3
i) 4.49 cm^3 to mm^3
j) 2.8 cm^2 to mm^2
k) 800 mm^2 to cm^2
l) 6.3 m^3 to cm^3
m) $57\,000 \text{ mm}^3$ to cm^3
n) 780 mm^2 to cm^2

EXERCISE 9.9 pt

1 The table shows six expressions: p, q and r are lengths. 5 and 2 are numbers and have no dimension.

$p + 2q + r$	p^2q^2	$2rq^2$	$\dfrac{pr^2}{q}$	$5pqr$	$2p(r + 5q)$

    a) Copy the table and put the letter A in the box underneath each of the **two** expressions that could represent an **area**.

    b) Put the letter V in the box underneath each of the **two** expressions that could represent a **volume**.

2 Here are three expressions.

Expression	Length	Area	Volume	None of these
$3\pi x + \pi y^2$				
$\pi z^2 + 2y^2$				
$\pi x^2 y$				

x, y and z are lengths. π and 3 are numbers and have no dimensions.

Copy the grid and put a tick ($\checkmark$) in the correct column to show whether the expression can be used for length, area, volume or none of these.

3 The expressions below can be used to calculate lengths, areas or volumes of some shapes. The letters b, w and h represent lengths. π and 3 are numbers and have no dimension. Pick out the **three** expressions that can be used to calculate a **volume**.

$bh + 3w$ $\dfrac{\pi}{3}bwh$ $\dfrac{bh}{3}$

$\dfrac{w^2h^2}{b}$ πb^2h^2 $\pi h(b^2 + 3wh)$

πbh $3\pi(bw + wh)$ $bh(\pi + 3)$ $3b^2 + 3bh$

4 Here are three expressions.

Expression	Length	Area	Volume	None of these
$6\pi b(2a + c)$				
$\dfrac{3ac}{\pi b}$				
$\pi a^2 + 2\pi b$				

a, b and c are lengths. $\pi, 2, 3$ and 6 are numbers and have no dimensions.
Copy the grid and put a tick (✓) in the correct column to show whether the expression can be used for length, area, volume or none of these.

5 Here are some expressions. The letters x, y, z and h represent lengths.
π and 10 are numbers that have no dimensions.
Three of the expressions could represent areas.
Copy the grid and tick (✓) the boxes underneath the three expressions which could represent areas.

$\pi(x + y + z)$	$10\pi xh$	$\pi x(10h + z)$	y^2z	$\dfrac{\pi x^2 h}{y}$	$10y^3z$	$\dfrac{\pi yz}{x}$

U3 CHAPTER 10

Pythagoras' theorem

EXERCISE 10.1

1 Look at these triangles, and use Pythagoras' theorem to decide whether they are right angled or not. The diagrams are not drawn to scale.

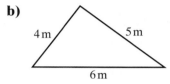

a) 5 cm, 6 cm, 8.5 cm

b) 4 m, 5 m, 6 m

c) 15 mm, 9 mm, 12 mm

2 For each of the triangles described below, use Pythagoras' theorem to decide whether it is right angled or not. If so, name the angle at which the right angle is located.
   a) AB = 9 cm   BC = 7 cm   CA = 5.4 cm
   b) AB = 2.5 cm   BC = 1.5 cm   CA = 2 cm
   c) AB = 8 mm   BC = 8 mm   CA = 11 mm
   d) PQ = 2.6 cm   QR = 3.5 cm   RP = 5 cm
   e) PQ = 2.5 m   QR = 6 m   RP = 6.5 m
   f) PQ = 7.2 cm   QR = 8.3 cm   RS = 12 cm
   g) AB = 15 km   BC = 20 km   CA = 25 km
   h) PQ = 2 mm   QR = 3 cm   PR = 5 cm

EXERCISE 10.2

1 Find the length of the hypotenuse represented by the letters *a* to *f* below. Give your answers to 3 significant figures.

2 Find the length of the diagonal of each rectangle.

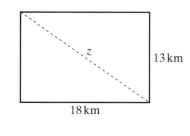

3 a) Find the length of **(i)** AB, **(ii)** BC.
   b) Hence find the length of AC.

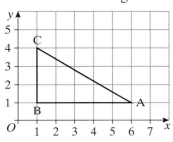

4 Find the length of DE.

EXERCISE 10.3 pt

1 Find the length of the sides marked *a* to *f* below.
   Give your answers to 3 significant figures.

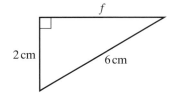

2 A rectangle has length 6 m and width *x* cm
   Its diagonal is of length 10 m
   Find the value of *x*

3 A ship sails due North for 8 km, then turns and sails due East for *y* km
   It ends up 15 km in a direct straight line from its starting point.
   Find the value of *y*

EXERCISE 10.4

1 Find the length of the side marked by the letters *a* to *f* below.
Give your answers to 3 significant figures where appropriate.

a)

a
3.6 cm
5.2 cm

b)

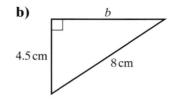

b
4.5 cm
8 cm

c)

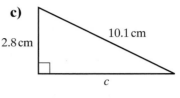

10.1 cm
2.8 cm
c

d)

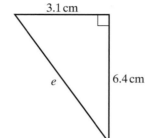

10 cm   10 cm
d

e)

3.1 cm
e
6.4 cm

f)

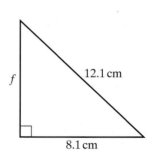

12.1 cm
f
8.1 cm

2 Find the length of the diagonals in these squares.

a)

7 cm

b)

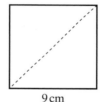

9 cm

3 a) Work out the height of this isosceles triangle.

13 cm
10 cm

b) Find the area of the triangle.

4 The diagram shows a rectangular field with a footpath running diagonally across it.
a) Work out the length of the footpath.

Ahmed walks from A to B and then from B to C.
Anthony walks from A to C along the footpath.
b) How much farther does Ahmed walk?

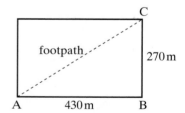

C
footpath
270 m
A   430 m   B

5 A man places a ladder against a wall.
The foot of the ladder is 3.4 m from the wall.
The top of the ladder is 2.7 m from the ground.
Work out the length of the ladder.

2.7 m
3.4 m

U3 CHAPTER 11

Transformations

EXERCISE 11.1

1 (i) Draw all the lines of symmetry on a copy of the following shapes.
(ii) Write down how many lines of symmetry each shape has.

a)

Rectangle

b)

Isosceles triangle

c)

Rhombus

d)

Parallelogram

e)

Trapezium

f)

Regular octagon

2 (i) Draw all the lines of symmetry on a copy of the following shapes.
(ii) Write down how many lines of symmetry each shape has.

a)

b)

c)

d)

3 Shade in squares on a copy of the following grids so that the resulting pattern is
symmetrical about the lines shown.

a)

b)

c)

d)   **e)**   **f)**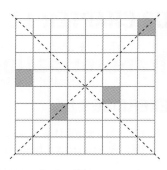

4 Sketch in a plane of symmetry on a copy of each of the following shapes:

a)

b)

c)

d)

5 Which of these shapes are **congruent**?

EXERCISE 11.2

In Questions **1** to **7**, on a copy draw the reflection of the given shape in the mirror line shown.
Label the mirror line with its equation in each case.

1

2

3

4

5

6

7
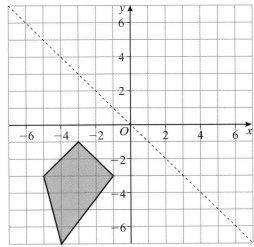

8 The diagram shows a triangle P and its mirror image Q.

    a) On a copy of the diagram, draw the mirror line that has been used for the reflection.

    b) Write down the equation of the mirror line.

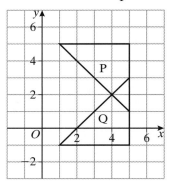

9 The diagram shows a triangle S and its mirror image T.

    a) On a copy of the diagram, draw the mirror line that has been used for the reflection.

    b) Write down the equation of the mirror line.

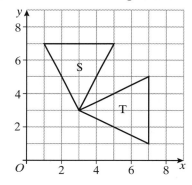

10 The diagram shows a letter T shape, labelled X.

The shape is to be reflected in a mirror line.

Part of the reflection has been drawn on the diagram.

    a) On a copy of the diagram, complete the drawing to show the image.

        Label it Y.

    b) Mark the mirror line.

    c) Give its equation.

11 The diagram shows ten triangles A, B, C, D, E, F, G, H, I and J.
The ten triangles are all congruent to each other.

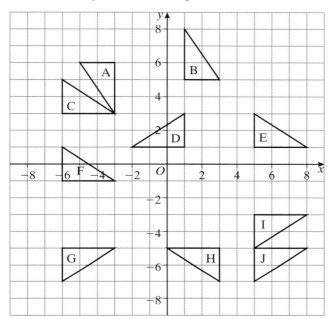

a) Explain the meaning of the word *congruent*.
b) Triangle E can be reflected to triangle I.
State the mirror line that achieves this.
c) Triangle H is reflected to another triangle using the mirror line $x = -1\frac{1}{2}$
Which one?
d) Triangle E can be reflected to triangle D using a mirror line.
Give the equation of this line.
e) Triangle B can be reflected to triangle E using a mirror line.
Give the equation of this line.
f) Triangle A can be reflected to triangle C using a mirror line.
Give the equation of this line.
g) Triangle G is reflected to another triangle using the mirror line $y = -3$
Which one?

12 A triangle P is reflected in the line
$x = 3$, to form an image, triangle Q.
Then triangle Q is reflected in the
same mirror line, to form an image,
triangle P.
What can you say about triangle P
and triangle Q?
Use a copy of the grid to help you.

EXERCISE 11.3

In Questions **1–4**, describe: **a)** the translation that takes A onto B

b) the translation that takes B onto A.

1

2

3

4

5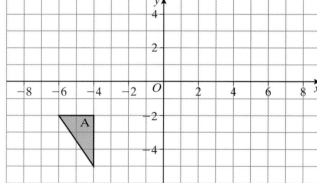

a) On a copy of the diagram, translate triangle A by the vector $\begin{pmatrix} 4 \\ 2 \end{pmatrix}$. Label the image B.

b) Translate triangle B by the vector $\begin{pmatrix} 5 \\ -1 \end{pmatrix}$

Label the image C.

c) Translate triangle C by the vector $\begin{pmatrix} -7 \\ 5 \end{pmatrix}$

Label the image D.

d) Describe the single translation that would take triangle D to triangle A.

6

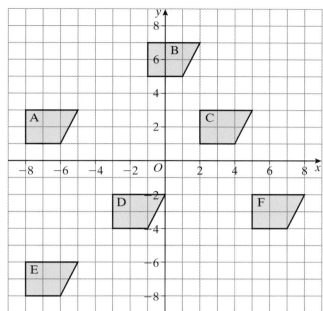

Describe the translation that takes the trapezium from:

a) A onto B   **b)** D onto F   **c)** D onto E   **d)** E onto A

e) E onto C   **f)** C onto B   **g)** A onto F   **h)** B onto D

EXERCISE 11.4

1 Write down the order of rotational symmetry of each of these shapes:

a)   **b)**   **c)**   **d)**

e)   **f)**   **g)**   **h)**

2 On a copy of this diagram, complete this shape so that is has two lines of symmetry and rotational symmetry of order 2

3 On two copies of this diagram, add one square to this shape so it has rotational symmetry of order 2
There are two possible solutions.
Draw each solution on a separate grid.

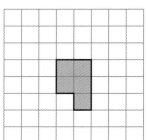

4 On a copy of this diagram, add three squares to this shape so that it has rotational symmetry of order 4

 EXERCISE 11.5

Use copies of the coordinate grids with x and y axes numbered from −8 to 8

1 Rotate the trapezium shape 90° clockwise, about O.

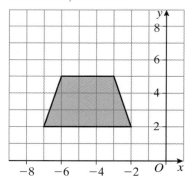

2 Rotate the L-shape by 180°, about O.

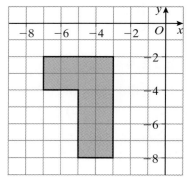

3 a) Rotate triangle T1 90° anticlockwise about O.
Label the result T2
  b) Rotate T2 180° about O.
Label the result T3
  c) Describe the single rotation that takes T1 directly to T3

4 **a)** Rotate triangle A 90° anticlockwise about $(0, 0)$
Label the result B.
   b) Rotate triangle B 180° about $(0, 0)$
Label the result C.
   c) Describe the single rotation that takes
triangle C to triangle A.

5

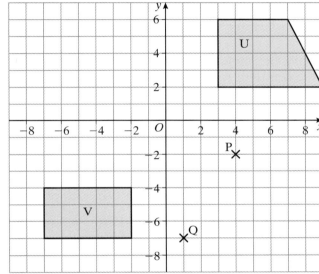

   a) Rotate shape U 90° anticlockwise about point P $(4, -2)$
   b) Rotate shape V 90° clockwise about point Q $(1, -7)$

6

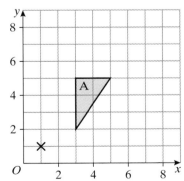

   a) Rotate triangle A 90° clockwise about $(1, 1)$. Label it B.
   b) Now rotate both triangle A and triangle B each by 180° about $(1, 1)$

7 The diagram shows an object A and its image B after a rotation.

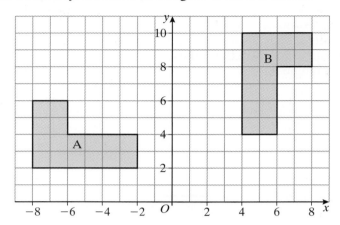

a) Write down the size and direction of the angle of rotation.
b) Write down the coordinates of the centre of rotation.

EXERCISE 11.6

Use copies of the coordinate grids with *x* and *y* axes numbered from −8 to 8

1 a) Reflect triangle S in the line $x = -1$
Label the new triangle T.
b) Reflect triangle T in the *x* axis.
Label the new triangle U.

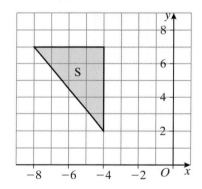

2 The diagram shows a triangle, T.

a) Translate triangle T by $\begin{pmatrix} 0 \\ 4 \end{pmatrix}$
Label its image U.

b) Rotate triangle U by 90° clockwise about *O*.
Label the resulting triangle V.

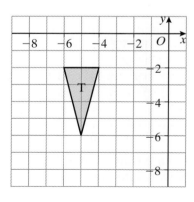

3 The diagram shows a triangle S.

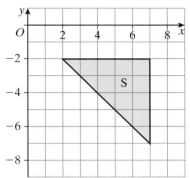

a) Reflect triangle S in the y axis. Label this image T.
b) Reflect triangle T in the line $y = -1$. Label this image U.

4 The diagram shows a rectangle. The rectangle is labelled F1

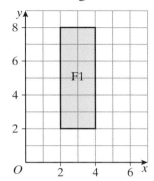

a) Reflect the rectangle F1 in the y axis. Label the result F2
b) Reflect F2 in the line $y = x$. Label the result F3

5 The diagram shows a quadrilateral E.

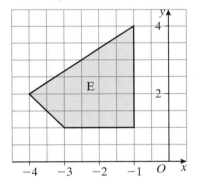

a) Rotate quadrilateral E through 90° clockwise about O. Label the result F.
b) Rotate quadrilateral F through 90° anticlockwise about $(1, -1)$. Label the result G.
c) Describe the translation that would take shape G to shape E.

6 The diagram shows a triangle P.

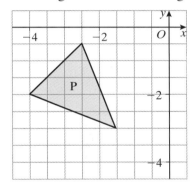

a) Rotate triangle P by 90° anticlockwise about $(0, 1)$. Label the result Q.
b) Reflect triangle P in the x axis. Label the image R.
c) Describe the translation that takes triangle R to triangle Q.

EXERCISE 11.7

Copy the following shapes in this Exercise onto squared paper.

1 Enlarge the following shapes by scale factor 2

a) **b)**

2 Enlarge the following shapes by scale factor 3

a) **b)**

3 Enlarge the following shapes by scale factor $\frac{1}{2}$

a) **b)**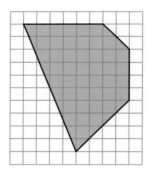

4 Enlarge the following shape by scale factor:

a) $\frac{1}{2}$ **b)** $1\frac{1}{2}$ **c)** 2 **d)** $2\frac{1}{2}$

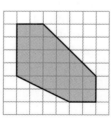

5 A shape has a perimeter of 16 cm.
Write down the perimeter of the shape when it is enlarged by a scale factor of:

a) 2 **b)** 4 **c)** $1\frac{1}{2}$ **d)** $\frac{1}{2}$

6 Write down which of these rectangles are:
   a) similar to
      (i) A   **(ii)** B   **(iii)** C
   b) congruent (there are three pairs).

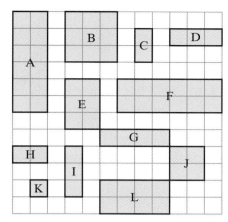

7 Which of these triangles are similar to
   triangle A?

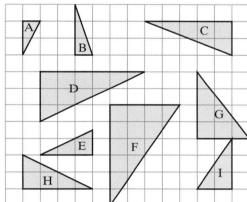

8 Are any two equilateral triangles similar?
   Give a reason for your answer.
   Use this diagram to help you.

9 Are any two rhombuses similar?
   Give a reason for your answer.
   Use this diagram to help you.

10 Are any two regular pentagons similar?
   Give a reason for your answer.
   Use this diagram to help you.

11 A triangle has angles of $110°$, $20°$ and $50°$
   Write down the angles in the triangle when it is enlarged by a scale factor of
   a) 2   **b)** $\frac{1}{2}$

12 a) Find the **(i)** perimeter, **(ii)** area of this rectangle.
The rectangle is enlarged by scale factor 3
   b) Write down:
   (i) the perimeter, **(ii)** the area of the enlarged rectangle.

8 cm

5 cm

13 a) Find the volume of this cuboid

3 cm

2 cm

5 cm

The cuboid is enlarged by scale factor 2
   b) Work out the volume of the enlarged cuboid.

EXERCISE 11.8 pt

For Questions 1, 2 and 3 in this Exercise, draw a copy of the grid.

1 The diagram shows a shape A.

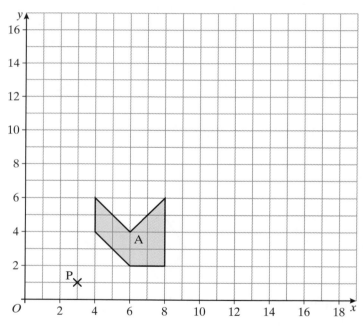

   a) Enlarge shape A by scale factor 2, centre P.
   Label the new shape B.
   b) Enlarge shape A by scale factor 3, centre P.
   Label the new shape C.
   c) State whether shapes B and C are:
   (i) congruent
   (ii) similar.

2 The diagram shows a trapezium.

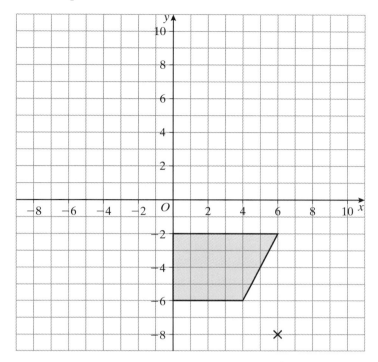

Enlarge the shape by scale factor $2\frac{1}{2}$, using centre $(6, -8)$

3 The diagram shows a shape, P, and two centres A and B marked with crosses.

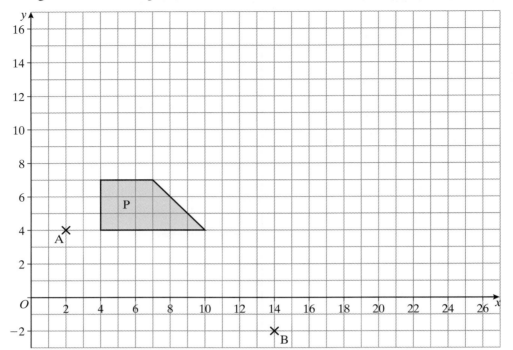

a) Enlarge shape P, with scale factor 3, centre A (2, 4)
Label the result Q.

b) Enlarge shape Q, with scale factor $\frac{1}{3}$, centre B (14, −2)
Label the result R.

c) State whether shapes P and Q are: **(i)** congruent   **(ii)** similar.

d) Are shapes P and R congruent?

4 The diagram shows an object, A, and the result B after an enlargement.

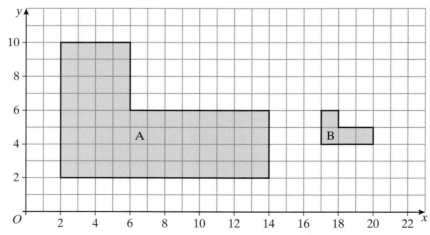

State the scale factor for the enlargement.

U3 CHAPTER 12

Constructions and loci

EXERCISE 12.1

In all your answers to this Exercise, you should leave all your construction lines showing.

1   Use ruler, compasses and protractors to construct these triangles.
    The diagrams are *not* accurately drawn.

a)

b)

c)

d)

e)

f)

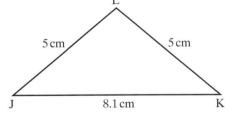

2   The sketch shows a triangle with
    AB = 73 mm, BC = 56 mm, AC = 87 mm
    Using ruler and compasses, make an
    accurate diagram of the triangle.

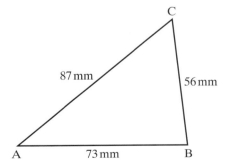

3 The sketch shows a triangle with AB = 84 mm,
BC = 52 mm and angle ACB = 90°
Using ruler and compasses, make an accurate
diagram of the triangle.

4 Draw triangle PQR with PQ = 8.1 cm, QR = 8.8 cm, angle RPQ = 90°
Use ruler and compasses to construct this triangle.
Show that there are two different solutions based on the given information.

5 Using compasses, try to make an accurate drawing of triangle EFG with sides
EF = 14 cm, EG = 6 cm, FG = 7 cm
What difficulty do you encounter? Find a reason for this.

EXERCISE 12.2

In all your answers to this Exercise, you should leave all your construction lines showing.

1 Use ruler and compasses to construct the perpendicular bisectors of these line segments.

a) A —————— 7 cm —————— B

b) A —————————— 12 cm —————————— B

c) A ——— 4 cm ——— B

d) A ———————— 9 cm ———————— B

e) A ————— 8.5 cm ————— B

2 Use ruler and compasses to construct the bisectors of these angles.

a) 60°

b) 36°

c) 80°

d) 54°

e) 110°

f) 25°

3 On a copy of the diagram, use ruler and compasses to construct the line from P perpendicular to the line segment AB.

×P

A   B

4 On a copy of the diagram, use ruler and compasses to construct the line from P perpendicular to the line segment AB.

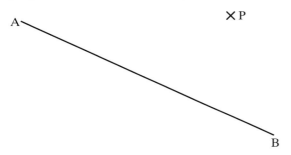
×P

5 On copies of the diagrams, use ruler and compasses to construct a line through P perpendicular to AB.

a)

A   P   B

b)

A   P   B

c)

A
P
B

6 a) Construct a triangle RST with sides
RT = 10 cm, RS = 13 cm, ST = 11 cm

b) (i) Construct the perpendicular
bisector of the side RS.
(ii) Construct the perpendicular
bisector of the side ST.
(iii) Construct the perpendicular
bisector of the side RT.
Your three bisectors should all meet at a
single point. Label this point X.

c) Draw a circle, centre X, that passes through R.
What do you notice?

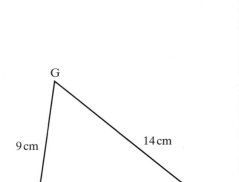

7 a) Construct a triangle EFG with sides
EF = 12 cm, FG = 14 cm, EG = 9 cm

b) (i) Bisect the angle EFG.
(ii) Bisect the angle FGE.
(iii) Bisect the angle GEF.
The three bisectors should
all meet at a single point.
Label this point Y.

c) Draw a circle, centre Y, that touches **one side**
of the triangle.
What do you notice?

8 Follow this method to construct an angle of exactly 150° without a protractor.

Step 1	Draw a line 7 centimetres long.
Step 2	Use this line as one side of an equilateral triangle.
	Use compasses and a straight edge to construct the other two sides.
	You now have three angles of 60°
Step 3	Choose one of the angles and bisect it.
	You now have an angle of 30°
Step 4	Extend one of the arms of the 30° angle.
	The angle next to the 30° will be 150°

9 Follow this method to construct an angle of exactly 135° without a protractor.

Step 1	Draw a line 8 centimetres long.
Step 2	Construct the perpendicular bisector of your line.
	You now have four angles of 90°
Step 3	Choose one of the angles and bisect it.
	The 90° angle together with one of the 45° angles makes 135°

In all your answers to this Exercise, you should leave all your construction lines showing.

1 Draw the locus of all the points which are exactly 5 cm away from the following:
  a)   •

  b) ————————————————————————
          8 cm

2 a) Mark a point P on your paper.
  b) Draw the locus of the points that are exactly 4.5 cm away from your point P.
  c) Shade the region that contains all the points *more than* 4.5 cm away from P.

3 a) Mark two points, C and D, 7 cm apart.   C •————————————————————————• D
  b) Draw the locus of the points that are equidistant from C and D.
  c) Shade the region that contains the points nearer to D than to C.

4 a) Mark two points, A and B, 10 cm apart on your paper.

      •   •
      A   B

  b) Draw the locus of the points which are equidistant from A and B.
  c) Shade the region that contains the points nearer to A than to B.

5 a) Mark two points, C and D, 8 cm apart on your paper.
  b) Draw the locus of the points which are exactly 2.3 cm away from your line.
  c) Shade the region which contains all the points *less than* 2.3 cm away from your line.

6 a) Use a protractor to draw two lines,
      PQ and PR at 50° to each other.
  b) Draw the locus of the points that are equidistant
      from the lines PQ and PR.
  c) Shade the region that contains the points nearer
      to PR than to PQ.

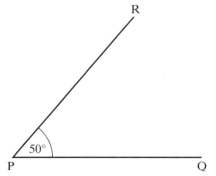

7 In the diagram, the rectangle
   represents a flowerbed.
   Poppy wants to make a path
   that is 2 m away from the edge
   of the flowerbed.
   Copy the diagram.
   Draw Poppy's path on your
   diagram.

Scale 1 cm to 1 m

8 a) Use a protractor to draw two lines, AB and AC at 72° to each other.

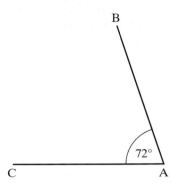

b) Draw the locus of the points which are equidistant from the lines AB and AC.
c) Shade the region which contains the points nearer to AB than to AC.

9 The vegetable patch in Josie's garden is rectangular in shape.

Josie wants to make a path around the *inside* of her vegetable patch.
She wants the path to be exactly 2 m wide and touching the perimeter of the vegetable patch.

a) Using a scale of 1 cm to 1 m, draw an accurate diagram of Josie's vegetable patch.
b) Accurately draw the path inside the vegetable patch.

10 In the diagram, the rectangle PQRS represents a farm.

It is to be divided up into three regions.
  The region formed by all points within 30 metres of PS will be the farm house.
  The region formed by all points within 40 metres of Q will be the hen house.
  The rest of the farm will be grass.
Using a scale of 1 cm to 10 m, construct rectangle PQRS, and indicate each of the three regions.

11 The diagram shows a rectangular nature reserve.
A gravel path is to be laid. The centre line of the path runs diagonally from E to G.
All parts of the nature reserve within 1 metre of this centre line are to be gravelled.

a) Using a scale of 1 cm to 2 m, construct rectangle EFGH, and mark the centre line of the path.

b) Shade the region to be gravelled.

A pond is to be built in the nature reserve.
The pond will occupy all points within 4.6 m of F.

c) Shade the area where the pond will be.

12 The diagram shows a paved play area at a school.

The local authority wants to erect a fence around the outside of the play area.
They decide that the fence should come to within 2 metres of the nearest point of the play area.
Using a scale of 1 cm to 2 m, make an accurate drawing to show the position of the fence.

13 The diagram shows a rectangular field ABCD.
Harry wants to bury some treasure in the field.

Harry buries the treasure exactly 3.5 m from DC, and exactly the same distance from AB and BC.
Using a scale of 1 cm to 1 m, construct rectangle ABCD and mark with a cross (×) where Harry buried the treasure.

14 At the edge of a bay there are three lighthouses. The diagram shows the position of the three lighthouses, P, Q and R.

Draw points P, Q and R quite far apart.

a) Using compasses and a straight edge, construct the locus of all points that are equidistant from P and Q.

b) Repeat the construction using Q and R, and again, using P and R.

c) Hence divide the bay into three regions, one for each lighthouse.

Use coloured pencils to mark the regions distinctly.

Land

EXERCISE 12.4

1 Match together these 3-D solids with their nets.

A   B   C   D

1   **2**

3   **4**

2 Which of these are nets of a cube?

A

B

C

D

E

F

3 On squared paper draw accurate nets of these solids:

a)
2 cm
Cube

b)
5 cm
1 cm
7 cm
Cuboid

c)
←3.5 cm→
8 cm
Cylinder
(circumference 11 cm)

d)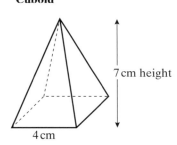
7 cm height
4 cm
Square-based pyramid

4 Sketch the 3-D shapes made by these nets.

a)

b)

c)

d)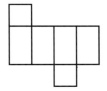

5 The isometric drawing shows some cubes forming a 3-D shape.
  a) Copy the shape onto isometric paper.
  b) On squared paper draw a sketch of
     (i) a plan view as seen from A
     (ii) a side elevation as seen from B
     (iii) a front elevation as seen from C.

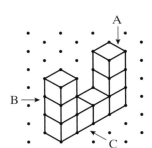

6 (i) Copy each of these 3-D shapes onto isometric paper.
  (ii) On squared paper, draw an accurate plan, front elevation (from A) and side elevation (from B) of each solid.
  (iii) Write down the volume of each shape.

 Represents 1 cm³

a)

b)

c)

d)

e)

f)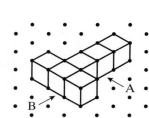

7 Here is a tin of sweets.
  The length of the label around the tin is 9 cm
  a) Draw an accurate net of the tin.
  b) Draw an accurate plan, front elevation and side elevations of the tin.

8 (i) Sketch each of these 3-D shapes onto isometric paper.
(ii) On squared paper draw an accurate plan, front elevation and side elevation of each of these solids:

a)

b)

c)

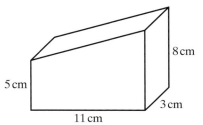

9 A pyramid has a square base whose sides are 5 cm long.
The triangular faces have sides 7 cm, 7 cm and 5 cm
a) Sketch a plan view of the pyramid.
b) Sketch a net for the pyramid.

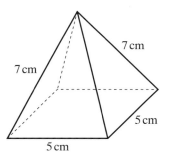

10 Kamini and Dakshesh have been building shapes with centimetre cubes on a square grid.
The diagrams show plan views of their shapes.
The numbers 1, 2, 3 tell you how many cubes are stacked on top of each square.

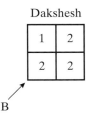

a) Draw a front elevation to show how Kamini's shape appears seen from direction A.
b) Make an isometric drawing of Dakshesh's shape, viewed from direction B.

11 Look at this cube.

  a) How many:
   (i) faces
   (ii) edges
   (iii) vertices does it have?

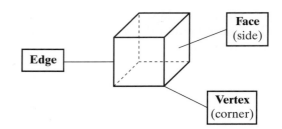

  b) Copy and complete this table:

Solid	Number of faces	Number of edges	Number of vertices	Number of faces + 2	Number of edges minus number of vertices
A					
B					
C					
D					
E					
F					

  c) What do you notice?